Gothic Fashion

The History

Gothic Fashion

The History

From Barbarians to Haute Couture

KATIE GODMAN

UNICORN

First published in 2022. This edition revised and
updated in 2024 by Unicorn Publishing Group
Charleston Suite, Meadow Business Centre
Lewes, East Sussex
BN8 5RW
www.unicornpublishing.org

10 9 8 7 6 5 4 3 2 1

ISBN 978-1-916846-10-4

Design by Matthew Wilson
Printed in India by Imprint Press

Contents

Introduction

What is Gothic Fashion?

———◆◆◆———

The twentieth century saw the rise of many subcultures, with 'goth' being one of the most instantly recognisable. The word 'goth' conjures up images of teenagers clad in dark colours with chunky boots, make-up-caked eyes and flowing clothes. The subculture is strongly associated with historical styles, tragic literature and moody music. Similarly, the word 'gothic' evokes shadowy hues, macabre tales and heavily decorated churches with elaborate graveyards to match.

Where do these ideas and associations come from? If a building is described as gothic, it is generally accepted that it is medieval, or, more commonly, Victorian in the style of medieval. Stories we think of as gothic often date from the nineteenth century, such as *Dracula* and *Frankenstein*, as well as the infamous penny dreadfuls. Just like Victorian architecture, these tales have their roots in more ancient times.

The Goths were originally an ancient European tribe. Throughout the 1600s, the word 'gothic' began to be used to describe styles from the medieval period. The 1700s saw the beginnings of popular gothic fiction (which tended to be melodramatic and historical). This in turn inspired gothic architecture and, by the early 1800s, fashion. The gothic look became one of the most common aesthetics we now associate with the Victorian era.

Goths, like most subcultures, evolved in the explosion of youth-obsessed society in the decades following the 1960s. They came of age in the 1980s, remaining part of the subculture spectrum to the present day with their Instagram-friendly extravagant clothes and bold colour choices. They have also spawned various subcultures of their own including cybergoths, psychobillies and steampunks.

Gothic fashion often draws on European traditions, blending different eras and folk costumes. Influences have recently come from further abroad, including horror films and gothic Lolita from Japan as well as skull motifs and Day of the Dead celebrations from Mexico.

Folk stories across continents and religions tell of the dead rising, monsters in the woods, lost souls feasting on the living and beings with magical powers. Throughout history these stories have been both

Gothic woman wearing a gown and a halo-like headdress, photographed by Sergei Kleshnev.

believed and dismissed, and treated with disgust and reverence; people have even died because of them. These ideas have always been with us and will probably continue to be so in some shape or form, horrifying and delighting us in equal measure, reflecting the darker side of the human psyche. They often come with their own imagined dress code, thanks to Hollywood films, book illustrations and the importance that society attaches to dress codes and colours, now influencing the fashion and style of modern goths.

Goths have influenced mainstream trends. Dark tulle, corsets, heavy boots and black coats with distinctive gothic flavours don't stay out of vogue for long. Famous fashion designers whose work has shown gothic influences include Vivienne Westwood, Alexander McQueen and Christian Lacroix.

Gothic style icons include burlesque performer Dita von Teese, British aristocrat Daphne Guinness, actress Helena Bonham Carter, rock star Dave Vanian, artist Bianca Xunise and comedian Noel Fielding, who all interpret the gothic style in their own way, from the playful to the stylish and everything in between.

The glamour of the past and the mystery of the occult holds an attraction for many people, and gothic fashion is one way to channel this. People have always romanticised the past, with Europeans traditionally viewing the Middle Ages as a lost golden age of folklore and beauty. Gothic fashion is more of a wishful amalgamation than a carbon copy of a genuine historical era, while the reinvention of past fashions is a practice common to all eras.

This book will chart the history of gothic fashion, beginning with its roots in the medieval period, to the present day, taking in arguably the most gothic century of them all: the nineteenth. It will examine the influences and evolution of gothic into the style we are so familiar with today. Whilst it will reference and chart gothic trends in music, art and literature, none of these elements are this book's primary focus. Gothic literature (especially from the nineteenth century) and goth music (especially from the 1980s) have been

Goth Friends in
Germany, 2017.

extensively written about in other publications. My aim here is to give an accessible overview of gothic fashion throughout history. The bibliography features texts which focus on other aspects of gothic culture. This book will mention other countries and cultures, but its focus will primarily be on the UK.

People come to gothic culture in various ways, through music, literature, film and social media, but also simply through an appreciation for the fashion – seeing a goth in the street or on the screen and wondering how to get that look. Unless you have no cultural context at all, you would probably realise that some elements of a goth's wardrobe reference mystical beings (such as cloaks being associated with vampires), or the darker side of life (for example black being associated with mourning).

Goth can mean different things to different people. It can often be used as a derogatory term, even by other subcultures. Goths can be portrayed as nerdy, or as devil worshippers, or as lonely and dangerous. There can be much media scaremongering, because goths appear more demonic than angelic. However, it hopefully goes without saying that if you are reading this book, you know that most goths are not evil serial killers! Similarly, whilst goth is a subculture that lends itself to the shy or the creative, not every goth is an introverted artist.

Some people actively set out to be a goth; others, when labelled as such, either embrace or reject the term; some might say they had a goth 'phase' or would describe themselves as 'a bit of a goth', and, while still not fully goth in dress, might still wear predominantly

Goth can mean different things to different people.

Dame Blanche, a
mythical French being.

Model on a catwalk at the
M'era Luna Festival in Germany, 2015.

dark colours or excessive eyeliner or chunky silver jewellery. In some cases, it is thought that certain people simply cannot be a goth because they don't like a certain band, while on the other hand, others mislabel people as goths simply because they have an alternative look. It is up to the individual to define themselves – or not – as they see fit.

For myself, I have dressed in goth fashion in some periods of my life more than others. I tend to be more gothic in winter than in summer (a fair-weather goth you could say), but I tend to mix in various styles that I like, including vintage, bohemian and historically influenced styles.

I was drawn to the gothic aesthetic because I like historical clothes and dramatic colours. I wanted to wear corsets, long skirts, long coats and boots, all of which chime with the goth aesthetic. I love lipstick, so I still wear bold lipsticks, and when I was a teenager, blue and black lipstick was one of the first 'alternative' fashions I experimented with. I have naturally long, dark-brown hair but it has been dyed black, green, blue, purple and red. I have an interest in gothic fiction, history, witches and the fantastical but don't have much stomach for actual horror.

My first awareness of goths was being very little and seeing a trio of what I now know as goths walking

past in velvets and lace, and just being stunned at how beautiful they looked. There were also elements of goth in my family. My mother wore Doc Marten boots and a long black coat when I was in primary school. My grandmother wears beautiful silver jewellery. My aunts had long dark hair, long coats and skirts, and one in particular, a fan of The Cure, helped me dye my hair and, in more recent times, accompanied me to Whitby.

Bristol, my hometown, is a city which embraces the bohemian and the alternative, with gothic buildings dotted about everywhere; it's also not too far from Glastonbury, with its abbey and mythical tor. In some

way, the gothic has long been a part of my life and I hope it long continues to be so.

Some people are quite stringent about what it takes to be goth, while others accept its fluidity and that it manifests itself in different ways in different people's lives. This book simply traces the history of gothic looks and examines how they have changed and evolved over time. It is an alternative subculture, and, historically, the definition of gothic is a broad church. By its very nature it attracts alternative and eccentric people, so in my opinion, it would be pretty strange if they all played by the same rules, since to reject the rules is, to some extent, why they're there in the first place.

pre 1750s

The Inspiration

Who were the original Goths? The answer lies in antiquity. It is widely accepted that they were notorious 'barbarians' who had a hand in ending the Roman Empire. They sacked Rome in AD 410, but before their interactions with the Romans, their origins are complicated and mysterious.

They are often described as a Germanic tribe, which means they could be of Central European or Scandinavian origin. There seems to more evidence to suggest they had links to Scandinavia and the Baltic Sea, making them kin to Vikings. Given the modern-day usage of the word 'goth' in terms of the subculture, the idea of the ancient Goths being similar to Vikings seems quite an easy and convenient notion, considering both modern goths and Vikings evoke ideas about paganism, blood and dark forests. In the contemporary media of the 2010s and early 2020s, portrayals of Vikings in film and television programmes certainly make them look like contemporary goths and punks, often sporting heavy eye make-up, spiky or messy hair and dark, layered robes and jewellery.

Geatland, which became Sweden in the Middle Ages, was home to the Geats. These people spoke old Norse and feature as Beowulf's clan in the famous legend. They were seafaring traders and had dealings throughout northern Europe. Even in the Middle Ages there is reference to the Geats living in Sweden. In ancient times, however, a group of Geats spread their wings.

These Geats came from Gotaland in Southern Sweden. It is thought that they left their homeland due to overpopulation and settled in Poland or the region now known as Ukraine for a time. It was these Geats who became known as the Goths. They do not appear to have had a written language, although they spoke Gothic, but they encountered literate peoples and so began to appear in Roman chronicles.

The Siege of Troy was wrongly attributed to the Goths by the Roman writer Jordanes. Both he and

A romanticised image of an ancient Goth.

another Roman author called Cassiodorus wrote chronicles of the Gothic people, but muddled their histories with other groups including the Danes and threw in bits of mythology to spice things up. Roman depictions of northern Europeans were as brutes and savages. The Goths did little to disprove these notions as they worked their way through the Mediterranean, plundering and pillaging until they found a place to settle. The Goths first clashed with the Romans in AD 238.

Little is known about the Goths before they encountered the Romans, which has made them easy prey for historians to depict as barbarians. By the 300s, they were practising a form of Christianity known as Arian, but eventually fell into line with the Catholicism practised in Rome. Tantalisingly, it is not known exactly what religion they practised before Christianity, which, given our modern interpretation of the word goth, gives licence for our imaginations to run wild with demonic and pagan notions. They probably practised some form of Norse paganism, given their origins.

Like many people in ancient Europe and the Roman Empire, they wore the sagum, a cloth which fastened across the body and was held together on the right shoulder with a pin or brooch which could be made from anything from fine metal and precious stones to animal bones and wood. Furs, animal pelts and fabrics made from wool as well as from plant fibres would have been worn, either keeping their natural colours or being dyed using natural methods involving vegetables, minerals or plants.

The most well known of the goth festivals is the Whitby Goth Weekend, started in 1994 by Jo Hampshire.

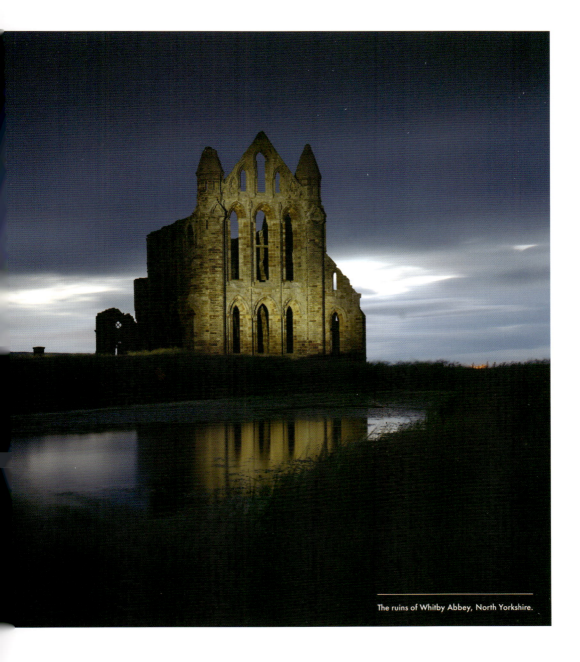

The ruins of Whitby Abbey, North Yorkshire.

Colours would have faded from constant wear, harsher lifestyles and the cleaning methods used on the naturally dyed fabric. Any notions the modern mind might conjure up of a Viking-like people striding around dressed head to toe in black would be false.

Relations between the Goths and the Romans varied, from some Goths becoming soldiers in the Roman army, to others unsuccessfully dabbling in Roman politics in AD 321 and 365 by supporting failed contenders for Emperor. One of the most significant encounters occurred when the Romans refused entry to the Goths after they were driven out of Ukraine by the Huns. The Romans humiliated the starving Goths by offering dog meat in exchange for making slaves of the Goths' children. Understandably, the Goths rose up, but when the Roman Emperor Valens led an army to stop them, he was defeated and killed. His successor Theodosius wisely chose to make peace, which lasted until AD 395.

The Goth tribes united under Alaric against the Roman Empire. After unsuccessful raids leading to a massacre of Goths in Constantinople, Alaric seized his chance after learning of weakness and infighting in the Roman government. He attacked Rome together with runaway slaves and supporters of the executed Roman general Stilicho. The Roman Empire was significantly weakened and would be attacked by other enemies over the next few decades. It was the beginning of the end for the most powerful empire of the ancient world.

After the Romans, the Goths lived throughout Dark-Ages Europe until the Middle Ages, with empires and kingdoms of their own, most notably in Gaul and Iberia (modern-day France, Spain and Portugal) where they established the Kingdom of the Visigoths; the Ostrogoths came to prominence in Italy in the fifth century. It seemed the Goths had settled down and begun to fit in with mainstream notions about being 'civilised'. They were eventually vanquished by other invading forces, such as the Byzantines and the Moors. Ironically, it was these little-known Gothic kingdoms which preserved Roman culture and Catholicism for future generations, and whose name, once a byword for barbarism, came to be associated with the style and architecture of Europe's medieval churches.

During the 1600s the word 'gothic' began to be used to describe the styles and architecture of the Middle Ages, mostly notably in continental Catholic churches, to differentiate from classical Greek or Roman style. The religious art and buildings associated with medieval Catholicism was lost to many British churches due to Henry VIII's Reformation of the 1500s, but was retained in the countries which had been part of the Goths' territory during the Dark Ages.

Examples of Gothic architecture in the UK include Whitby Abbey, Salisbury Cathedral, Glastonbury Abbey and Westminster Abbey. Much architecture from the nineteenth century was designed intentionally in the gothic style, mimicking these earlier buildings and known as Gothic revival. Features in Gothic buildings include arches, gargoyles and vaulted ceilings. Gothic architecture celebrates and beautifies the bones of the buildings whereas other styles tend to cover them up.

This usage was then applied to other aesthetic elements of the Dark Ages and the medieval period. This included art works, music (especially choral music such as Gregorian chant) and fashion styles. In more modern times, this can also include buildings, clothes and artwork up to the sixteenth century (for example certain Tudor fashions), or from later eras which were influenced by these periods. These Gothic designs are often bold and elaborate, in contrast to the clean, classic designs of the Romans and Greeks. They still heavily inform our ideas about gothic fashion and style today.

HISTORY OF THE COLOUR BLACK

Black clothing brings to mind grief and mourning; however, it has had other connotations throughout history. It was often tied to the church. Throughout European history, the Catholic Church was very wealthy. Priests', monks' and nuns' vestments were often black, and while this may seem merely functional to the modern eye, in medieval times it was seen as ostentatious.

It is costly and time-consuming to dye a fabric dark black and keep it that way. Washing, scrubbing and leaving to dry in the sun can cause dark garments to quickly fade, especially as the colour would have been derived from natural dyes. Black dye can be made from the root and bark of alder, chestnut and walnut trees. Iron salt was used to deepen the colour, but this also damaged the fabric. Another method was to first dye the fabric dark blue using woad, and then to add red dye from the madder root; this would generally produce black, but having to dye an item twice was time-consuming.

Wearing black for prolonged periods of mourning did not become widespread until the nineteenth century, but more on the mourning cult of the Victorian era in a later chapter. Wearing black at medieval funerals was by no means commonplace, especially if the deceased was not of noble birth. One of the reasons for this was simply that people owned fewer clothes, as well as the difficulty and expense of dyeing. The Industrial Revolution made it cheaper to manufacture clothes, but before this time, it was unusual even for the wealthy to own many items of clothing. It simply wouldn't have been practical or affordable to buy a whole black mourning wardrobe. Historically, the lower classes wore their darkest coloured clothes or donned a dark cape (in the 1500s) or a scarf (in the 1600s) on the day of a funeral. This evolved through the tying of black crepe on top hats in the Victorian era to wearing black armbands on uniforms or suits in the twentieth century.

Periods of mourning were observed for different times and for different periods throughout history. Black has been associated with mourning since the ancient Greeks, although, in medieval times, or even later, in the Renaissance, it was often more about signifying status. Black was not only the chosen colour of the clergy but also that of the professional classes such as doctors and lawyers, who wore black robes and jackets.

Another method was to first dye the fabric dark blue using woad, and then to add red dye from the madder root.

Philip the Good, Duke of Burgundy, after Rogier Van Der Weyden, c.1445.

Black was not the only mourning colour available: white was commonly worn for the death of a child or an unmarried woman until the 1800s, or by French widows. Romany communities wore red. In the nineteenth century, red was worn by those still in mourning who wished to attend a wedding. Purple was reserved for royal mourning until the 1800s, when it came to signify the later stages of mourning.

Mourning fabric could not be shiny; it was believed reflections could trap the spirits of the dead. This was why mirrors were often covered during periods of mourning. Because of this, poplin was used in the 1700s for the first stage of mourning, and then black silk after three months. Crepe or linen could be used if it had no shine, as could bombazine. This fabric, a blend of silk and wool, has largely fallen out of use. For prolonged periods of mourning it was ideal, as it was hardwearing and lacked shine.

Wearing black as a sign of wealth was popularised by Philip the Good, Duke of Burgundy (1396–1467). He became duke after his father was assassinated; he wore black for the rest of his life not only to mark this but also to display his personal wealth and that of his court, which became known as a fashionable and sophisticated centre of art and culture. This fashion then spread to European upper-class society as a whole.

The Spanish royal family were famed for wearing black in the sixteenth century, so much so that a shade was called 'Spanish Black'. Spain was also the site of the former Kingdom of the Visigoths. The Spanish

Portrait of Catherine de Medici,
after François Clouet, c.1580.

royal family had links with the Burgundian royal family as well as the Holy Roman Empire and the papacy. The Holy Roman Emperor Charles V (1500–1558) and his son, King Philip II of Spain (1527–1598) usually wore black, probably a nod to clerical vestments. It was believed at this time that the monarchy was ordained by God – kings ruled by divine right, and wearing black helped to underline this point.

Other royals associated with black include Catherine de Medici (1519–1589), the Italian-born Queen of France who wore it rather theatrically for the rest of her life after her husband's death in 1559. She is often portrayed as an evil figure due to her role in the St Bartholomew's Day Massacre. Mary I (also known as Bloody Mary) is also portrayed as wearing black, perhaps due to her Spanish husband, Philip II. At her execution, Mary Queen of Scots wore a black gown which she removed revealing a red petticoat and bodice underneath. These queens have bad reputations, so the association with them may be one of the reasons why black outfits have villainous connotations to this day.

Pale skin was another sign of wealth in the medieval and Renaissance world; it was evidence you didn't work in the fields and could afford a life of luxury. Elizabeth I famously wore white make-up to emphasise this, establishing the archetype of the pale English rose for generations to come, and providing a classic look for the heroines of gothic novels and modern-day goths.

The first example of mourning jewellery gaining popularity was in 1649, after Charles I was executed. The Royalists (his followers) incorporated miniature portraits or locks of his hair into their rings with the slogan 'The glory of England has Departed'. By the end of the century, it was increasingly common for the wealthy to distribute memorial rings to friends and family following a death. They often used a skull or bones as part of the decoration and were made of stones such as Whitby jet, pearls, bone or black glass. By the nineteenth century, roses, praying hands, weeping silhouettes and urns were also used in designs.

In some medieval societies, wedding dresses amongst the nobility were often dark; as mentioned above, dyeing and keeping colours dark was expensive, so this was another opportunity to display one's wealth. A costly wedding celebration in medieval times was not the norm: it was a definite statement of wealth and power.

Black can be used to symbolise piety; despite its expense, it became linked to the Puritans in the 1600s. Dutch merchants at that time, despite being incredibly wealthy, wore black to give the impression of being strict Protestants.

Black can effectively offset white lace or golden jewellery and suits fine fabrics such as velvet. With it being used by the clergy and the upper classes, it quickly became a colour which imbued authority upon its wearer, especially if it was well kept.

As it can be seen as a non-colour, black can even suggest that the wearer doesn't care for trivialities such as fashion. Black matches everything; it is simple, plain, strong and business-like. Yet surely this suggests that the wearer cares more about fashion than they are letting on. If they really aren't bothered, why not wear orange or green? Of course not: black means power because of its intense history connected to grief, authority, royalty and religion.

Purple and red have also become associated with gothic fashion. As previously mentioned, purple is connected to mourning, as well as nobility and royalty. Imperial Purple, also known as Tyrian Purple, was obtained from Mediterranean sea snails. Due to its bright colour and surprising colour-fastness, it was the most coveted and expensive dye in Europe in classical times. For centuries it was reserved only for royalty or nobility. This tradition was started by ancient Greeks and Romans and intermittently enforced by subsequent societies via sumptuary laws (enforced dress codes for different levels of society) throughout European history. The word 'purple' itself was sometimes used instead of 'blood' in Tudor England, and therefore suggested death. In Western culture, red has signified blood and danger but also has connotations of royalty. Overall, colours associated with the gothic aesthetic are often opulent.

GOTHIC STYLES

From the 1800s, the term 'gothic' started to be applied to fashion styles influenced by historical clothing. Gothic clothing of the twentieth and twenty-first centuries acknowledges nineteenth-century fashion, which in turn was influenced by Elizabethan, medieval and Renaissance fashion.

Sleeves

Billowing sleeves are commonplace in modern gothic fashion. They are linked in the public imagination with the medieval period, and particularly princesses, knights, magic and witchcraft. In the Middle Ages, they were part of the attire of wealthy men and women. The use of the extra fabric would have been a way to show off one's wealth, as well as to provide warmth.

These sleeves were not just part of one garment, as is often the case today. An under robe or chemise for women or a shirt / under tunic / doublet for men would be the first layer. A kirtle would be worn over it, sometimes in a contrasting fabric, as it was often intended to be displayed as part of the dress design, such as the fitted under-layer of the sleeve, or seen through a slit in the skirt. The outer layer would then feature decoration and the drooping sleeves.

These final, outer layers had various names and styles throughout history. For women, these included various types of robes: the bliaut (featuring pleated skirts and sleeves with a high neck, worn in the twelfth century); the cotehardie (with flared skirts trailing on the ground and sleeves finishing at the elbow before

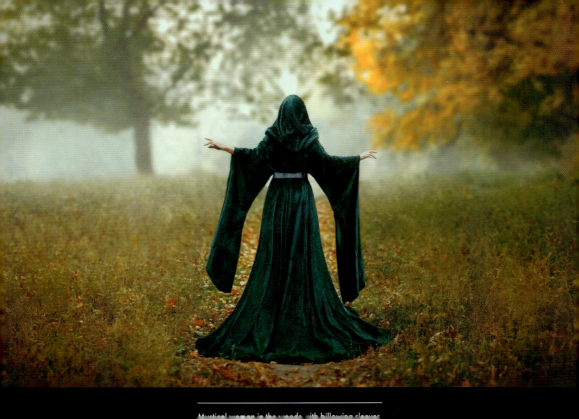

Mystical woman in the woods, with billowing sleeves

Portrait of Lysbeth van Duvenvoorde, anonymous, c.1430, Rijksmuseum.

dropping to a long, thin point, worn in the fourteenth century); and the houppelande (very voluminous, high-waisted and high-necked, with huge trailing sleeves, worn in the fifteenth century). Men's outer garments were often similar, but shorter, to reveal their hose-clad legs. These exaggerated sleeves went in and out of fashion for much of the Middle Ages. By the mid-sixteenth century, they tended to be stiffer and more structured and more likely to be lined with fur (with the outer garment often being called a gown). In the late sixteenth century, puffed sleeves overtook billowing, drooping sleeves as the fashionable choice.

To the modern eye, the many layers worn in previous centuries can look cumbersome and uncomfortable, but it is worth remembering that from the fourteenth to the nineteenth centuries, the globe experienced what is known as a little ice age; before the days of global warming, this meant it was much colder. Long sleeves would often be made from fur and other thick materials to help insulate the wearer.

Another type of sleeve associated with the gothic look is the puffed and slashed sleeve. This did exist in the medieval period but only really came to the fore in the sixteenth century.

Puff sleeves, like billowing sleeves, were also a way of displaying wealth. They required extra fabric, as well as, in some cases, extra hidden material to support them and maintain their 'puff'. Slashed sleeves were

Portrait of a Young Man, Aelbert Cuyp, c.1651, Rijksmuseum. Black, slashed sleeves showing cream fabric underneath. Both colours would have been hard to maintain in the seventeenth century and were therefore a sign of wealth.

Doublet, early 1620s, Metropolitan Museum of Art.

also popular. The top layer was stylishly slashed to reveal the layers underneath. Both layers were made from extremely expensive fabrics, often in contrasting colours or textures to really help them stand out.

Statement sleeves exist in other cultures, but perhaps would not have been called gothic until very recently, when they have been incorporated into Western gothic fashion. For example the Japanese kimono – an ancient garment worn by both men and women – tends to have voluminous sleeves. As in the West, this excess of fabric was to show off wealth, but was also thought to ward off evil spirits and could be used in dance.

Portrait of a Young Lady, unknown artist, 1567. A young lady with many tiny slashes and contrasting fabric peeking through, in a very painstaking and decadent design.

The back lacing of a twenty-first-century corset, worn as an outer garment and a fashion statement.

Corsets

A corset is an iconic garment, adored by contemporary goths and fashionistas alike for its ability (to an even greater extent than billowing sleeves) to conjure ideas about bygone eras, romance, grandeur and feminine glamour. However, the history of the corset is widely misunderstood and misrepresented. It has changed and evolved dramatically over the centuries, depending on the fashionable shapes of the time and tailoring technology. For one thing, it hasn't always been called a corset ...

The Minoans were the first culture believed to have worn a corset-like garment. They lived on Crete and are the oldest civilisation in Europe, predating even the ancient Greeks. Their surviving paintings and statues show Minoan women wearing long, wide skirts, with thin waists cinched by a girdle or short-sleeved corselet which finished under the breasts, leaving them exposed. It appears the Minoans did not think this scandalous at all, as they depicted goddesses and queens in the same way, and it appeared to be the accepted form of courtly dress. Men also wore similar garments, for support during their favourite sport of bull-jumping.

Artwork from the Mycenaean society, the Minoans' contemporaries on mainland Greece, show corsets made of metal plates which could have been used as armour. The ancient Greeks themselves used leather bands as shapewear.

The corset then doesn't make much of an appearance for several hundred years. During the

medieval period, corsets were not generally worn, contrary to popular belief. Many clothes were held in place by being laced up, giving the impression of a corset to the modern eye, but it was an era which predated zips and when buttons were an expensive luxury. Contemporary gothic fashion often uses lacing in this way, or sometimes as a decorative flourish, perhaps hiding a zip. In medieval times, external laces were often used to fasten garments or keep them together; this was then sometimes exaggerated for design purposes.

In the same era, bodices and undergarments were form-fitting and sometimes made of stiffer fabric to provide support, but perhaps more akin to a tight-fitting vest than a corset. Chaucer mentions the word, but it is thought this could have meant any sort of garment for the torso. Corsets only began to be properly introduced in the fifteenth and sixteenth centuries, and the corset we know today only really appeared in the nineteenth century. Historically, they have been called by various names: bodices, 'a pair of bodies', jumps, stays or corps.

Jumps were generally shorter and laced at the front for women who didn't have servants to help them. Stays (or a pair of bodies) developed gradually and had a more practical purpose than just squeezing a tiny waist: they were used as support garments before the invention of elastic. They only began to be used to distort the body in the sixteenth century, making the waist smaller and pushing up the bosom. Stays were in two halves which laced together. The neckline of gowns went up and down dramatically in the sixteenth century,

Italian corset, 1770s,
Metropolitan Museum of Art

becoming very low and emphasising the bosom by the Elizabethan age – a look helped by stays.

During the early sixteenth century, undergarments began to incorporate more serious shapewear. Both men and women wore boiled leather bodices under their clothes. Spanish and Italian fashion began to introduce garments with stiffening materials much more like the corsets we recognise today. They were used to reshape both men and women, making them look slender by smoothing out any lumps, as well as actually flattening the breasts.

By the late 1500s, whalebone was much in demand amongst the elite for stiffening 'bodies' or bodices. Along with other stiff materials such as horn, wood or metal, whalebone did not completely encircle the garment but was inserted in the front of the bodice and secured in place. Known as busks, these were intended to maintain an upright posture; it's important to note that they were removable, so it was possible to only wear them when receiving visitors. They were sometimes inscribed with saucy love notes and images, acknowledging they had been given to the lady by an admirer or partner, with the couple happy in the secret that she would be keeping a memento close to her heart – and between her breasts.

The supposed widespread use of steel corsets in this period, worn by the likes of Catherine de Medici and Elizabeth I, is actually a myth and was only confined to the elite. However, it became important for the upper classes to move with grace and dignity, and corsets helped to make this second nature.

The eighteenth century saw an iconic trend for tight stays, with some of the most outlandish fashions ever seen making their appearance in Western society. A thin waist with heaving bosoms was a must. The outer layer of the robe or gown often revealed a decorative bodice, or a panel called a stomacher worn over the top of the bodice in a contrasting colour.

The Regency period saw the shape of dresses change again, this time to neoclassical styles. Stays became more like push-up bras. The Romantic and gothic fashions of the 1820s onwards called for small waists, so longer stays were back in fashion, but were now known as corsets.

Until the nineteenth century, these various forms of corsets had sleeves or straps, sometimes removable and attached with string or ribbon. The corset developed further in the nineteenth century as a sleeveless garment. Jean Julian Josselin invented the clamp form corset in 1829, with laces at the back, but metal clamps at the front. This style of corset is still popular today, often worn as outerwear.

The use of medical corsets was common across history. Before the availability of elastic and other stretchy and supportive synthetic materials, garments were used to support breasts and stomach muscles and improve posture. Our ancestors suffered from many (to them) unexplainable illnesses and deformities, many of which would be easily cured now with improved diet, more exposure to sunlight and medical treatment of congenital conditions. It was believed that using supportive garments to strength

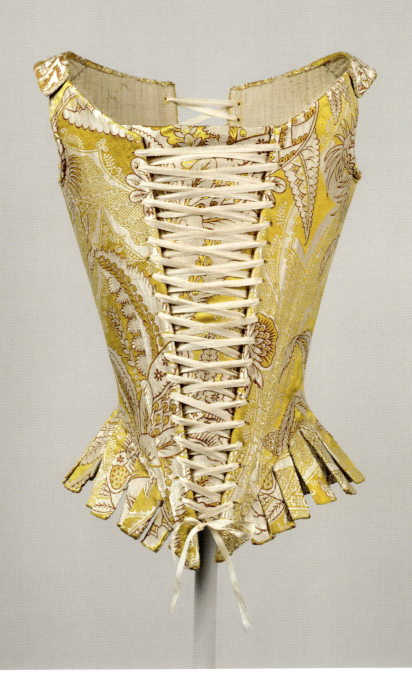

Anne of Denmark,
John De Critz the Elder,
c.1605–1610.

the body would help, and children of both sexes were often trained to wear corsets.

This may have been of some help, especially at a time when women became pregnant more often, affecting breasts, stomach muscles and backs. It is a fallacy, however, that many women and girls were tightly laced into corsets of metal and bone throughout history. The practice was recognised as early as the sixteenth century as being unhealthy for expectant mothers. In Elizabethan, Georgian and Victorian times, a small waist was prized, but generally, stories about thirteen-inch waists and continuous fainting fits are exaggerated.

Form-fitting, stiffened bodices were no less uncomfortable than bras or control-top knickers, rather than the instruments of torture or fetishist devices we sometimes imagine them to be. As a parallel, extremely high-heeled stiletto shoes do exist today, but this does not mean that most women are forced to wear them every day. Corsets have suffered from a bad reputation since the sixteenth century, for allowing women to lie about their figure and as an example of the extremes they will go to for the sake of vanity, to look thin and to seduce men. On the other hand, a woman not wearing the correct underwear for her time was equally scorned – indeed, this is where the phrase 'loose woman' is thought to have come from – a woman without a corset.

Farthingale

A farthingale was a hooped petticoat. It originated in sixteenth-century Spain and spread through the royal courts of Europe. It gave the wearer the appearance of a cylindrical skirt. Lower-class women attempted to imitate this voluminous silhouette using bum rolls: padding tied at the waist making the skirts flare out. The farthingale was a forerunner of the pannier, worn in the eighteenth century, which extended the width of the skirts at the side, and the crinoline and bustle from the nineteenth century which made skirts bell-shaped and emphasised a protruding back, respectively. These garments add drama to any outfit, but also make movement more difficult and perhaps allude to the damsel in distress so beloved of old gothic tropes. When exposed, they can look strangely skeletal and alien, adding to their gothic appeal.

Conch

These wing-like items, made from wire and covered in sheer fabric, were worn on the most extravagant Elizabethan gowns. They arch out from behind the collar and almost frame the wearer, often extending to the floor. They were not for everyday use but for high-status women dressing to impress. They give the wearer an otherworldly, ghostly, slightly fae appearance. In an interesting quirk of history, Shakespeare lodged with the Mountjoy family while

working on *Othello*. Christopher Mountjoy was a tire maker —a skilled craftsman who made conches, amongst other things. In the so-called Golden Age of Elizabethan England, fashion was big business. Many Huguenot refugees found a home in England and worked as silk weavers or conch makers, bringing exciting continental fashions within tantalisingly easy reach of the English nobility.

Cloaks

Cloaks have been with us since the earliest times: seemingly simple garments, available since man learnt to skin an animal and decided to drape the hide upon himself, but they have since become much more sophisticated. Different societies have cut and draped capes in unique ways, keeping them in place with ties, brooches and everything else in between.

Initially a practical garment for protection from the elements (with the added bonus of doubling as a blanket), they quickly became more embellished. An essential garment for venturing outside in northern Europe, they naturally came to be used to communicate something about the wearer. In prehistoric times, fastenings were made from beautiful natural items such as shells and stones. The Romans and Celts often used gemstones, with the Vikings and

Elizabeth I of England, workshop of Nicholas Hilliard, c.1599.

A cloak adds mystery and protection to the wearer.

Anglo-Saxons making large brooches out of glass. From being made from hide, cloaks developed to wool and then to being woven from tweed-like fabrics and trimmed with fur. They were both practical and eye-catching, a quick and easy way to convey status when the wearer was out and about. In ancient Rome, the colours and lengths of cloaks often represented the status of the wearer: low-ranking Roman soldiers wore red cloaks, while generals wore purple.

Cloaks became even more intricately decorated throughout the Renaissance world, and capes appeared: shorter cloaks with less practical use. In Elizabeth I's court, shorter capes with fancy collars were fashionable, with embroidery and lining. One such cape features in the story of Sir Walter Raleigh offering to protect Queen Elizabeth's feet from a muddy puddle by laying his cape over it. Both men and women continued to wear long cloaks for warmth. They were often cut in a circular shape, made of thick fabrics such as wool or velvet and lined with hoods. The rich made brooches and clasps from valuable metals and gemstones.

The cloak is versatile for both rich and poor, depending on which fabric is used.

As the use of farthingales and panniers also became fashionable, cloaks needed to become bigger to cover the unnaturally wide skirts. Velvet was incorporated into the design of more decorative cloaks during the Renaissance and remains synonymous with them to this day.

Cloaks are highly theatrical garments; when hooded, they can conceal the wearer's identity, making them useful for the plots of tales of mistaken identity, murder, intrigue, spying and forbidden love. Their usually dark colour only adds to their mysterious appeal. This theatricality has helped them to survive in gothic fashion in the present day, when their usefulness has been rendered superfluous by modern fabrics, central heating and form-fitting coats.

The cloak is versatile for both rich and poor, depending on which fabric is used. They fit all shapes and sizes, as well as protecting fashionable wider skirts from bad weather. Men and women continued to wear cloaks until the nineteenth century, when men began to wear coats instead. They remained popular with women, especially when skirts became very wide in the 1850s. Some were long and practical, while others were shorter and richly decorated, sometimes trimmed with fur.

Cloaks reaching the waist are often known as capes, with shorter cloaks covering the shoulders known as mantles. By the early twentieth century, cloaks had gone out of fashion for both men and women, though capes still formed part of a nurse's uniform. They have gone in and out of fashion through the 1960s and 1970s, as well as into the 2010s and within the goth subculture. Cloaks *can* be worn today for special occasions.

Ruffs

Ruffs are hard to emulate, even with modern fabrics, and are very impractical. They relate very specifically to the sixteenth and early seventeenth centuries, but are often referenced in gothic fashion, and help to transport the reader back in time in gothic novels and films.

A modern re-imagining of a
Renaissance outfit complete with a ruff.

Portrait Miniature,
Oliver Isaac,
1590, V&A.

They were made from starched fabric and were a sign of opulence and wealth due to the work required to maintain them: they definitely required the assistance of a servant. They came in different shapes and sizes, from fully surrounding the neck to framing the face around the shoulders. They were big business. Elizabeth I was often likened to a fairy queen because she wore one; she looked unnatural and not of this world, already hinting at their later gothic use. They also appear frequently in the sombre and reserved Dutch fashions of the sixteenth century. Combined with black clothing, they had an air of gravity and understated opulence to contemporary eyes, but a very gothic look to the modern eye.

When Elizabeth I ascended the throne in 1558, she ushered in an era of stability and prosperity. She was a very glamorous queen with a love of fashion. Big ruffs became fashionable for both sexes, with some over 40cm in diameter. The development of starch (or the 'devil's liquor', as the Puritans called it) allowed ruffs to remain stiff when worn. They could be worn with different outfits; some were so large that wire and strings were needed to keep them standing up. You had to be careful not to get caught in the rain – if they got wet, they would become floppy!

Religious upheavals on the continent led to a large influx of immigrants into Protestant Britain. They brought their trades, such as embroidery and headdress-making, with them, contributing to Britain's booming fashion market. The invention of the spinning wheel sped up the production of clothes and fabrics. At the same time, explorers were travelling the world and bringing back exotic jewels, feathers, fur and fabrics, all of which influenced fashion.

The ruff was popular throughout Europe; variations of it can still be seen today in European folk costumes, for example, in Brittany.

Ruffs evolved into the Medici collar by the end of the sixteenth century (named after Catherine de Medici), which were almost like half-ruffs which opened at the neck. In the seventeenth century, large, flat collars, or falling collars, later known as vandyke collars because the famous seventeenth-century artist painted so many sitters wearing them, became the extravagant neck wear of choice.

Jewellery

Much contemporary goth jewellery tends to be silver rather than gold. This could perhaps reflect a desire to buck the mainstream trend, or to mimic the moon and stars in the night sky; or perhaps it takes its inspiration from ancient European jewellery, especially Celtic designs, which were similar to those used by the ancient Goths. This style is often silver or metallic. Again, to the modern eye, it evokes a bygone age of mysticism, which is probably why it appeals so much to goths.

Portrait of a Lady with a Ruff, Michiel Jansz. van Mierevelt, 1638, National Gallery of Art.

Woman wearing a Renaissance-inspired choker.

Jewellery was very popular during the Renaissance and the sixteenth century, especially rings, earrings and necklaces on both women and men, something again favoured by the goth community. The eighteenth century saw the widespread popularity of choker necklaces, continuing into the nineteenth century; in the 1890s, they were made from lace and covered the entire neck. Chokers have gothic connotations, their link with the neck suggesting macabre meanings, such as beheadings or vampires.

Jewels of choice for goths tend to be darker or more dramatic, such as jet or rubies; crystals are also popular, due to their association with healing and well-being, as are faux gems made from glass in various dark hues, and pearls, especially black ones. As well as silver, the dark metal titanium is also favoured by goths.

Veils

Veils tend to be worn by women for religious and cultural reasons to preserve their modesty. In ancient Greece, women had to be veiled at all times in public: to be unveiled was a clear signal you were a prostitute.

Many Islamic women today choose to cover their heads with veil-like garments called hijabs.

In Europe, widows have worn veils since medieval times to appear humble in their grief, as well as possibly to shield themselves from the gaze of other men. Historically, veils have been long and almost cloak-like, mysteriously concealing the wearer and adding a sense of enigmatic glamour around them.

They also bear comparison to nuns' habits, as well as to the black-lace veils called mantillas that Spanish ladies would use to cover their heads for Mass.

They are also associated with the pivotal moment at a wedding when the groom pulls back the bride's veil, hoping to be greeted by a beautiful woman – but then, with gothic, who can really know for sure what awaits him!

Pointed Shoes

From the fourteenth to sixteenth centuries, pointy shoes were highly fashionable. They were a decadent display of wealth – they were not only costly to make, but proof that you had servants; they were so impractical and difficult to wear that you needed other people to carry out even the most basic tasks!

They were worn by men and women; the points were sometimes so long that they curled up and were tied to the leg. The Church disapproved of such frivolous fashion trends; it's believed by some that they were seen as sinful because they made kneeling in church difficult! They came to be known as 'Satan's claws' because of their shape, and it wasn't long before they became associated with tricky fairies and witches.

In the 1980s, pointed shoes were known as winkle pickers and were very much associated with goths of that era.

Gothic Armour

The classic full helmet-to-boots armour (including armour for the horses!) was developed in the Holy Roman Empire (modern-day Germany) in the fifteenth century. It was highly detailed and has heavily influenced both male and female gothic dress, including items that include metalwork such as jewellery, fastenings, belts and corsets.

GOTHIC FIGURES
Witches

Modern goths draw inspiration for their looks from characters from folklore, which often seemed very real to people in the past – witches are a particularly heavy influence, with #witchygoth being very popular on Instagram.

Illustration from *The Strange and wonderful history of Mother Shipton*, 1686.

For centuries, people truly believed that witches were evil beings. Stereotypically, they were older women who tended to live alone. They were more likely wise women, brewers (also known as ale witches) and herbalists, commonplace across rural Britain before medical practice was standardised (and masculinised) during the eighteenth and nineteenth centuries. Their herbal remedies could easily be seen as potions. The medical establishment and the patriarchy, in general, were unhappy that these women provided cures from the land, so it was easier to vilify them.

While witches were burned throughout the medieval period, it was later, during the seventeenth century, that executions became most common. With civil war, religious strife and suspicion raging across the country, perhaps it should be no surprise that resentment and fear ruled people's minds.

There were wise women and priestesses in many ancient societies; unsurprising, perhaps, given that pantheistic religions worshipped many goddesses. Women sometimes acted as interpreters for the gods, by reading runes and conveying messages.

Our idea of how witches and wise women look and dress derives from a cross-section of many different eras; their appearance has been popularised by Hollywood films such as *The Wizard of Oz*. Many different ideas about witches' attire have fused together.

They are often portrayed as wearing black – probably a later invention linked to older women as widows in mourning clothes. Wise women in medieval times may well have worn darker clothes for practical

purposes, as they may have grown the various ingredients for their medicines on the land.

The pointed hat could have several origins. The oldest example comes from the discovery of the mummies of three Chinese women who lived in the third or fourth centuries BC. They are known as the Witches of Subeshi, as they were found wearing tall felt hats, believed to have been worn by shamans. Since they lived near the Silk Road, it is entirely possible that ideas about shamans wearing such hats could have travelled to Europe. These mummies were unearthed in the 1970s, when the image of witches wearing tall, pointed hats had already become embedded in popular culture: perhaps we are guilty of projecting non-existent meaning back into the past. However, such a striking article of clothing would suggest status of some kind; perhaps these women held some sort of magical or advisory role within the community. They were buried with each other, not with men, suggesting their status was different from any of the normal roles we might expect from those times – they were not simply the wives or mothers of rich men.

It was fashionable in medieval Europe for rich ladies to wear pointed hats called hennins. Like pointed shoes, they were an impractical show of wealth; like many over-the-top fashions, they were easily vilified due to their obvious decadence, which was applied in turn to the wearer.

Another famous example of the pointed black hat is the various depictions of Mother Shipton throughout history. She was a Tudor prophetess who was believed to be a witch and to have the power of correctly uttering predictions and curses. Eighty years after her death, her predictions were written down in a book. She is sometimes known as the British Nostradamus, as it is believed she correctly predicted the Second World War and the invention of the internet. A dark brown moth has been named after her: witches are often associated with animals, generally those with darker colouring or who have magical powers already attributed to them. These include cats, bats, crows, magpies and moths.

The Puritans and Quakers of the seventeenth century also wore tall, wide-brimmed hats; after the Pilgrim Fathers travelled to the New World, they became associated with hysterical witch hunts and trials in places such as Salem during this period. Welsh folk costume encompasses a tall black hat. It is thought these were adopted from the tall hats worn by Puritan and Quaker communities in the 1600s.

Maria di Portinari, Hans Memling, 1470.
This finely dressed lady wears a hennin.

The broomstick is a stereotypical tool used by a working woman and a homemaker. To 'jump the broom' was also a symbolic act at weddings, and has been credited to both West African and Welsh culture. It is most well known as a way for enslaved people in America to marry without permission from their master or the services of a priest. These traditions suggest the humble broomstick has sacred powers. The popular image of witches riding broomsticks is linked to ideas of promiscuity, especially given the placement of the broom handle!

Many legends exist about shape-shifting witches and magical women such as sirens using their magic to lure men to their doom; perhaps this is why young, attractive witches seem to be desirable style icons. Long flowing robes are also often associated with magical people, particularly in reference to some generic ancient time.

Another classic dress code (or lack of it!) associated with witches is nudity. In *The Crucible*, young women famously sneak off into the forest to shed their clothes and inhibitions and conjure havoc. However, this was enshrined in folklore (and in some 'magical' practices) long before Arthur Miller. Young, naked witches act as counterpoints to the image of the old hag, giving witches their sex appeal.

Being a witch, soothsayer or priestess often gives women a subversive role in society – a strange position of authority or knowledge which is often forbidden to them, and which they may use for good or evil. It is a highly compelling narrative.

Vampires

Vampires are another gothic style icon, although the idea of a glamorous, elegant vampire only arose in the nineteenth century with the publication of John Polidori's novel *The Vampyre* – but more on that later.

Vampires, or vampire-like creatures, were first mentioned in the *Epic of Gilgamesh* from the second and third millennia BC. Vampires are believed to need to drink the blood of a living person to survive, the victim then dying or becoming a vampire themselves. The vampire has eternal life – both a blessing and a curse – and can only be killed by (most commonly) a stake through the heart. They also have an aversion to religious imagery, especially crosses. Interestingly, crosses existed as a design long before the advent of Christianity, and only began to be used by Christians in the seventh century.

Vampires have been given different powers in many different cultures and narratives, from flight to shape-shifting, from hypnosis to the power to control crows. Thanks to modern popular culture, it's now believed they can turn into a bat, that they have no reflection, are unable to enter a building unless invited, are unable to stand the sun, can hover and have super strength. Storytellers cherry-pick elements and invent their own sorts of vampires. It was often believed vampires had pale skin, hinting of their undead, bloodless state and their lives lived in shadow. Their pointed canine teeth, which can extend into fangs to suck blood, are ever-present.

In modern fiction, vampires tend to use seduction to attract their victims. In earlier times, vampires were

Female vampire in medieval-inspired dress.

more like zombies: shambling horrors. Most cultures do tell of the dead rising, sometimes exactly as they were when alive, but more often as terrifying shadows of themselves, with a will to harm the living. The veil between the living and the dead has often seemed thin, and the desire or fear of breaching it has gripped the public imagination. Skulls and bones feature heavily in gothic fashion in reference to this, as does, arguably, pale skin, with its connotations of ghosts and its deathly pallor! Myths about vampires are said to have arisen from various misunderstood illnesses, such as rabies and even the Black Death, which could leave bloody pustules around the mouth.

Bram Stoker's *Dracula*, continuing the idea of the noble vampire established by Polidori, is believed to have been inspired by Vlad the Impaler, a fifteenth-century Romanian nobleman. He was considered a hero by many for defending his ancestral lands from the Ottoman Empire, but was better known for cruelly impaling thousands of his enemies on stakes to die, and then supposedly dipping bread in their blood.

Elizabeth Bathory (1560–1614) was another genuine historical figure to have inspired vampire lore, a member of the ruling elite of Transylvania. She has often been called the most prolific female serial killer in history. Using her powerful position, she tortured and killed countless young women, mostly servants or young girls sent to her for an introduction into noble circles, purportedly so she could bathe in their blood and preserve her own youth. Shielded by her wealth and protected in her castle, it was a long time before she was brought to justice. Her servant accomplices

The idea of vampires
being of noble birth
dates only from the
nineteenth century

A modern interpretation of fae.

were executed, but she was walled up in her castle under lock and key until her death. The idea of vampires being of noble birth dates only from the nineteenth century, but the vampire is a suitable metaphor for the nobility, protected by their high status and castle walls and not being held accountable for their crimes.

Most of our ideas about vampiric dress sense are based on the fashion of the elite, particularly the nineteenth century, when the myth was standardised. However, a range of historical clothes have become associated with vampires because, in theory, anyone can turn into one, whether rich or poor. As their immortal nature became part of the myth, however, so too did the idea of rich vampires amassing fortunes over the centuries. They are often depicted wearing a cloak, helpful for flying and very dramatic if they shape-shift into a bat. The nineteenth-century noble vampire is now a commonly accepted image.

Ghosts

Ghosts are believed to be the spirits and souls of the dead, come back to walk the earth. Most cultures believe in them. They are often depicted as shadowy beings, all in white or grey. Their influence on gothic fashion is clear, from the deathly pallor of their skin to their clothing. They are often said to wear what they died in, so in folklore they appear dressed in clothes from past eras, or wear a floating death shroud which can act as a cloak.

Zombies

Zombies are another form of undead being. They are re-animated, rotting dead bodies. Whereas a ghost may retain their personality, zombies are mere monsters out to terrorise the living. Popularised by Hollywood films, they probably derive from an amalgamation of various folklore traditions.

In the Philippines, the Aswang look like ghosts but act more like zombies, hunting for babies to devour. In European folklore, a ghoul is a zombie-like creature which lives in graveyards. In The Gambia, the Kikiyaon is reputed to hunt human souls, and is human in appearance, aside from its wings. The zombies we know from the cinema are misrepresentation of Haitian culture by Hollywood where voodoo priests bring back the dead to act as their mindless slaves.

In modern times, it is believed that zombie legends derive from tragic misunderstandings about victims of severe accidents who are left with life-changing brain damage, or those suffering from forms of mental illness such as catatonic shock.

Fae

Various forms of fae, or fairy folk, exist all over the world. More recently, Hollywood films and children's stories have depicted them as kind, sweet beings. In earlier mythology they were seen as mischievous or even wicked, tricking humans and having to be appeased with treats. Fairies, pixies and elves are some of the most popular examples. They are often shown with butterfly-like wings, thin, elegant (sometimes elongated) features and long hair. Whilst their dress doesn't tend to be darkly coloured, it is often inspired by medieval garments, such as long sleeves and skirts. They are often seen to be wearing Celtic-style jewellery – all of this giving us an idea of what a 'magical' being should look like.

These motifs and trends derive from ancient times and have continued through the Middle Ages and the Renaissance. The word 'gothic' was not used in the Middle Ages, even though most of these trends emerged during that period. It only began to be applied in the seventeen century, initially to architecture and then, gradually, to fashion from the late eighteenth century. It also meant 'uncivilised' and 'barbarian', so it wasn't originally applied to medieval buildings as a compliment. The meaning of the word expanded, and thus the medieval period is often seen today as being dark and gloomy. When applied to clothing, 'gothic' refers to style trends from the medieval period through to the sixteenth century which are transplanted onto modern contemporary fashions.

Of course, there is another era which, arguably, has the most influence on modern gothic fashion: the Victorian. Victorians also drew on past fashions, and rather enjoyed a macabre and gloomy culture often associated with the goths of today. But, of course, the Regency period came first – a time often associated with light colours and classical styles but also when people first started dressing in a consciously gothic fashion, setting a trend for the goths to follow.

1750s–1830s

The Rise of Gothic and Romanticism

Horace Walpole is credited with writing the first gothic novel, *The Castle of Otranto*, in 1764. It was called 'gothic' because of its historical setting, a plot involving a haunted castle and its sinister, superstitious feel. Many other authors followed in his footsteps, and the publishing industry churned out countless gothic novels over the following decades.

Horace Walpole's home, Strawberry Hill, was transformed into a gothic mansion with a series of renovations inspired by medieval palaces and churches. His trendsetting helped ignite a taste for the gothic in the public imagination, which would gather pace over the coming decades. The novels which populated the gothic genre reinforced the idea of Catholic Europe as being lost in the past and filled with horrors, dangerous mythology and villains, as opposed to the safe modernity of Protestant Britain.

Gothic novels skyrocketed in popularity during the late eighteenth and early nineteenth centuries. Arguably, they were the original fiction genre, mixing elements of history, horror, mystery, romance and sometimes even erotica. Many were set on the continent (often in places the authors had not visited) in unspecified time periods that were generically medieval or Renaissance. The authors were predominantly female, and some, such as Ann Radcliffe and Rosa Matilda (a pseudonym for Charlotte Dacre) became household names, and their young female readership had a huge appetite for the escapism these books offered. While the novels reached their peak in the 1820s, much of the literature and culture of the nineteenth century would continue to be influenced by them. Other novelists, such as Matthew Lewis, who wrote *The Monk*, pushed the boundaries of decency by developing the more horrific aspects of the gothic genre, whereas Radcliffe tended to be more romantic, with the frightening elements of her books being more suggestive than explicit.

The splendour of the consciously
gothic Strawberry Hill Interior.

Illustration from Ann Radcliffe's *The Mysteries of Udolpho*, 1794, British Library. The author, Ann Radcliffe, made her fortune from gothic novels. Her books had European and historical settings, although she wrote most of them before she travelled abroad.

The Nightmare,
Henry Fuseli, 1781,
Detroit Institute of Arts

In the late 1700s, gothic (or 'gothik' as it was sometimes spelt) novels created a hunger for plays and artwork. Painters such as Henry Fuseli and Francisco Goya are well known for the disturbing and melodramatic works they produced during this time. Gothic novels were often not very thoroughly researched, and neither were the clothes worn in paintings and plays. Many of the costumes were based on contemporary fashions, so the actors and models could still look glamorous by the standards of the time (as still happens today), with historical flourishes such as helmets, ruffs, cloaks, and vandyke collars. To Georgian eyes, this look harked back to the English Civil War, a time just about far enough out of reach of living memory that it could be deemed romantic. The Golden Age of Elizabeth was also in vogue, driven by a zeal for patriotism as the British Empire expanded. Likewise, the French romanticised Elizabeth's contemporary, Henry IV.

Fuelled by public interest in all things Elizabethan (including women's dresses with their low-cut necklines and wide skirts), Alderman John Boydell opened a Shakespeare Gallery on Pall Mall in 1789 and published an accompanying book. The gallery housed 170 paintings by artists including Henry Fuseli, depicting pivotal Shakespearean scenes. Like gothic paintings, plays and novels, the costumes depicted were a glorious mishmash of dramatic historical clothes and contemporary fashion. There was some criticism of this abandonment of historical accuracy for the sake of style, but it did little to dissuade these trendsetters, who, over the coming years, would take these historically-inspired looks from the world of art into the streets and homes of Britain.

Lady Macbeth Seizes the Daggers by Henry Fuseli.
Note the puffed sleeves on Lady Macbeth's gown.

THE REGENCY

By the end of the eighteenth century, changes in politics and technology dramatically transformed the way people lived. Revolutions in France and America had seen monarchies not only questioned but also overthrown. The Industrial Revolution (1760–1840) allowed fabrics to be produced quickly and cheaply, creating fortunes and destroying cottage industries; cities expanded at an alarming rate.

While, for many, the Industrial Revolution meant relocation to the cities to find work in the harsh environment of factories, it made others rich. Many of the successful factory owners came from the working rather than the upper classes. This contributed to the growth of the middle class at the turn of the nineteenth century, changing British society and fashion forever. More people could afford to dress fashionably, so fashion began to change at a faster rate, fuelled not only by industry but also a growing circulation of magazines (such as *The Lady's Monthly Museum* and *La Belle Assemblée*).

This era is often referred to as the Regency. Technically, the Regency period runs from 1811 to 1820 when the Prince of Wales acted as Regent during the illness of his father, King George III. However, the term is often used to encompass the stylistic traits of the late

Napoleon's first wife Josephine De Beauharnais (1763–1814) wearing a very simple Regency gown inspired by the classical world of the ancient Greeks and Romans.

REGENCY FASHION GLOSSARY

Spencer: Short jacket worn by a lady.

Pelisse: A lady's long, thin coat.

Bateau neckline: Off the shoulder.

Chemise dress: A forerunner to the neoclassical-style dress, it takes its name from the underwear it was thought to resemble.

Georgian period, from approximately 1795 to 1830. The aesthetic associated with this period is known as neoclassical, since ancient Roman and Greek styles provided much of the inspiration for the simple, elegant architecture and women's fashion.

More people than ever were learning to read as a result of the expansion of the middle classes. As a result, novels grew in popularity; they captured the imagination of young women, and the development of fantastical genres fed their imaginations.

Much has been written on how the neoclassical-style Regency gowns became fashionable. There was a desire to throw off the excess that was seen to have fuelled the French Revolution, including the over-the-top fashions of the eighteenth century. Archaeological discoveries from the ancient Greek and Roman worlds also fuelled interest in toga-like garments. This style of fashion is often portrayed as being more egalitarian, influenced as it is by simple togas, chemises and peasant dresses.

The Regency can be viewed as an experimental period still processing the fallout from the French Revolution and other social shifts. The Napoleonic Wars also dominated much of the era, and, throughout history, periods of conflict or strife can be connected with artistic experimentation, such as the 1920s after the First World War. During the Regency, there was a flurry of activity from painters such as J.M.W. Turner and the publication of works from some of the best-known writers in the English language, including Jane Austen, John Keats, Lord Byron and

Mary and Percy Shelley, some from the increasingly important middle classes. There was a leaning towards liberal ideas – the transatlantic slave trade was abolished in 1807; in more Bohemian circles, there were ideas about 'free love' and there was even the beginnings of an animal rights movement.

One of the most important years for the history of the gothic was 1816, known as the year without a summer. The eruption of Mount Tamboro in Indonesia in April 1815 was so powerful it affected weather and climate patterns around the world for the next few years, especially in 1816. Harvests were poor in Europe, and the nights drew in earlier. Lord Byron, John Polidori, Percy Shelley and Mary Godwin Shelley chose this year to tour Europe. Bad weather left them holed up at the Villa Diodati, where, after a party game, Mary Shelley wrote *Frankenstein* and Polidori wrote *The Vampyre*.

REGENCY GOTHS

It is during this period that gothic fashion, as we might recognise it today, started to appear, with people consciously incorporating historical fashions into contemporary dress. Fashions had always been recycled and inspired by the past, but this era seems to be the first time the word 'gothic' was used to

Fashion Plates from 1814, showing the trends moving away from simplicity to gothic style flourish such as the puffed sleeves, V&A.

fashion. Neoclassical dresses were closer to medieval styles in shape, but this did not prevent a blending of styles from various historical periods. The most common embellishments were puffed, faux-slashed sleeves and extra details on the hems, as well as embellishment on the bust. Other examples included braiding, faux corset-style lacing and foliage. As the nineteenth century progressed, gothic fashions also began to include lower waistlines. They borrowed and blended from the various medieval, Tudor, Stuart and Renaissance periods which provided the settings for gothic novels.

Many of the early Regency gothic-style dresses were white, perhaps because of its association with purity – often a characteristic of gothic heroines – or perhaps simply due to the influence of the popular neoclassical gowns of the time, which tended to be white, as they were influenced by the dress of the ancient world. White could also have macabre connotations: it was worn in mourning after the death of a child or young woman (i.e. a virgin). In addition, and perhaps even more ghoulish, Marie Antoinette was executed wearing a white chemise dress, prompting a craze for young women to cut their hair and to combine white dresses with red necklaces to reference the victims of the guillotine. There were

describe this process; many of those wearing it were young women encouraged by the gloomy, fantastical and spooky fiction they were reading, as well as the plays they watched and the paintings they viewed. Sound familiar?

The unspecified time periods and settings of many of these works of art allowed not only the authors but also the fans much poetic licence; like cosplayers today, they were only too keen to emulate the styles worn by their favourite characters.

Given the popularity of gothic novels, it was probably inevitable that they would influence Regency

Portrait of a Woman, Henry Inman, c.1825,
Brooklyn Museum.

Jacoba Vetter, Charles Howard Hodges, c.1821–1825,
Rijksmuseum. Note the ruff, as well as the puffed detailed
sleeves – a dress clearly inspired by the Tudor period.

even rumours of wigs being made from the hair of the freshly beheaded.

Thin, white chemise dresses were also thought to cause illness, especially consumption (or tuberculosis, as we know it today). Doctors of the time, perhaps incorrectly, cited them as a cause of death in women taking fashion too far in a bid to look like their swooning, fictional gothic counterparts. Contracting consumption was romanticised as a genteel death

and made to seem attractive, as one of its side effects was pale, ghostly skin and shining eyes. The fact that it took such a long time to kill you also provided ample opportunity for romantic lamenting!

Many of the white gothic dresses and pelisses were ornately decorated with large collars reminiscent of the seventeenth century, heavy embroidery, ruffs, frills and flounces on the hem and puffed sleeves. The embroidery is an example of 'whitework' embroidery,

Portrait of Emma Jane Hodges, Charles Howard Hodges, c.1810, Rijksmuseum. wearing a high-necked gown complete with a floaty-looking ruff – more like a frilled collar.

Mary Lodge, Bride of Baron Charles-Louis de Keverberg de Kessel, Joseph-François Ducq, 1818, Musea Brugge / Groeningemuseum.

a style of needlework native to Ayrshire and a popular cottage industry there until the 1830s. Wearing this style of embroidery could have been seen as a nod to more traditional industries, placing even greater emphasis on the historical elements of this style.

Ruffs were part of the gothic style, featuring in contemporary fashion plates. Given the time and effort it probably took to maintain them, they were often saved for ballgowns or worn only by the very wealthy.

Many dresses and pelisses, however, had frilled collars – similar in appearance to ruffs, but much easier to maintain.

By the 1810s, Regency gothic fashion was growing in popularity, and many of the originally simple neoclassical gowns were showing some level of embellishment. More varied colours and prints were also being used, as well as heavier fabrics, a contrast to the pale muslins of the early Regency period.

Pelisse, c.1820, American, Metropolitan Museum of Art.
Detail showing military-style brocade and buttons.

MILITARY STYLE

Different ornamentations were nods to different interests, so gothic trimmings were a sign that the wearer enjoyed contemporary literature and was interested in history. Military embellishments, as well as displaying patriotism, could also show support for a male relation holding a prestigious military position. Military ornamentation, especially braiding, was often combined with gothic styles and still features in gothic fashion today.

The Napoleonic Wars lasted from 1799 to 1815, ending with the Battle of Waterloo. They included conflicts such as the Peninsular War (1807–14) in which Britain, along with various changing allies, fought to prevent Napoleonic France from increasing its grip on the continent. Many young men joined

up to fight: officer commissions in the army had to be paid for, so were effectively only available to the wealthy. Naval officer commissions provided a cheaper alternative, as they were free if you could pass a written test. While this still barred many lower-class men due to their lack of education, it did mean men from middle-class families could become officers. It was an officer's responsibility to employ his own tailor to make his uniforms. With dashing young men sporting buttoned and braided military jackets, the style had an impact on the fashions of the day.

Women's clothes began to feature military-style braiding and buttons. Many women wished to show support for the men who had joined up; or perhaps they were simply envious of their stylish jackets! The embellishments were usually worn over women's outer layers, such as pelisses and spencers, just as they were on men's jackets. The style became extremely popular in the 1810s in the run-up to Waterloo.

Perhaps gothic and military styles were combined because, as the soldiers could be viewed as knights in shining armour, the clothes offered another chance to indulge in fantasy; or perhaps a link could be made between the gothic and patriotism, as British female royals often featured as gothic heroines. Then again, perhaps they simply looked good together.

MOURNING

One of the most obvious types of gothic attire is mourning wear. Due to the increasing circulation of magazines, and the upper classes needing to affirm their place in society in a fast-changing world, mourning wear became more socially regulated during the Regency period. Non-shiny fabrics such as crepe, bombazine, poplin and linens were deemed more appropriate, different lengths of mourning were set for different family members and different stages of mourning allowed for a gradual move from black through to greys and purples.

The upper classes could afford to have new mourning clothes made, turning the increasingly compulsory process of mourning into a show of wealth. The middle classes, keen as ever to emulate their supposed betters, and with magazines keeping them informed, began to recycle old clothes for mourning dress. While mourning would not be expected on every occasion, Jane Austen's letters mention the passing

away of so many acquaintances that it's not much of a stretch to think that, at any given time, several members of the average middle-class social circle would have been wearing mourning clothes. Austen wrote that 'my mourning will not impoverish me' and her letters mention how the middle classes kept up with mourning fashions without breaking the bank, often by dyeing, relining or completely restructuring old clothes.

The textile industry tried to manufacture a myth that it was bad luck to reuse mourning clothes each time someone died. Their intention was obviously to drive up trade by encouraging people to purchase new mourning clothes on every occasion, but given that people tended to own less clothes than we do now, this would have been a highly extravagant practice. Mourning clothes even reached the lower classes; servants were given them on the death of their employers, and charities were established to lend them out for funerals.

As previously mentioned, white was also used for mourning in the eighteenth century, especially on the death of a woman or a child. This extended into the Regency period, especially in the later stages of mourning when it was combined with black. White was very popular in the neoclassical styles of the early 1800s, the functional and gothic dresses doubling as mourning clothes.

In 1817, Princess Charlotte, the popular heir to the throne, died along with her baby after a fifty-two-hour labour. She was the only legitimate child of the Prince Regent. (Had she and her baby survived, her cousin

Study of a Woman, Marie-Denise Villers, 1802. This early nineteenth-century portrait of Madame Soustras shows the subject putting on her shoes. She is dressed in black and even wearing a black veil, so appears to be in mourning, despite her informal pose. It would have been highly unusual for a young lady to wear black in any other context during this period.

Victoria would never have been crowned and there would have been no Victorians). Her untimely death led to widespread public mourning.

The first stage of mourning at court was to last two months; during this period, the nobility had to wear undecorated black clothes in dull fabrics. Greys and purples were allowed at a later stage. Where the royal court led, the middle class followed – with tremendous

enthusiasm, given Princess Charlotte's popularity. So many people went into mourning that contemporary magazines ran fashion plates in mourning styles and colours, making darker colours and heavier fabrics seem more fashionable and attractive. It was said that people at court bought entirely new wardrobes because the official mourning period was so long. This level of public mourning was unprecedented.

Mourning dress, from Ackermann's
Repository of Arts, British Museum, 1811.

MOURNING DRESS.

Madame Jacques-Louis Leblanc, Jean-Auguste Dominique Ingres,
1823, Metropolitan Museum of Art. Madame Jacques-Louis
Leblanc is wearing black, most likely for mourning. The gothic style
is obvious in the decorated bodice, puffed sleeves and additional
ribbons and sheer fabric. This was a deliberate display of wealth,
as the look would have been expensive to maintain. By the 1820s,
the neoclassical gowns' the waists of neoclassical gowns had
started to drop, leading to a more Tudor and Elizabethan-style
silhouette, with smaller waist and wider skirts.

Mourning dress, c.1820, British, Metropolitan Museum of Art.

Arguably, the 1810s first saw a link between darker fabrics and gothic styles, at a time when gothic embellishments were increasingly becoming part of mainstream fashion. Many people, especially fashionable young women, would have already been in mourning in the early 1810s because of the high number of fatalities suffered during the Napoleonic Wars. Jane Austen mentions the wars in her letters; in 1811, she laments: 'How horrible it is to have so many people killed!' The Napoleonic Wars saw the largest loss of life amongst British soldiers until the First World War.

Increasingly strict mourning etiquette, and the large-scale mourning seen during the Napoleonic Wars and after the death of Princess Charlotte, can be seen as significant reasons for the shifting mood during the later Regency to a more sombre look. Given its subject matter, this probably led to an increased taste for the gothic, which strongly influenced the change in styles.

KEEPING UP APPEARANCES

Another reason for the rise in gothic trends was clothing's increased ability to support gothic embellishments. The neoclassical dresses fashionable in the early 1800s did not fasten at the back (illogical as this may seem to us), but with strings and pins in an apron style. This made them fairly flimsy, but by the 1810s, buttoning up at the back started to catch on. The fronts of the dresses became more robust and able to support more ornamentation. The busts and sleeves of dresses could now be puffed, appliquéd and ruffled – all in exciting, gothic styles.

Mourning dress, c.1820, British, Metropolitan Museum of Art.

The gothic style was a useful way to show wealth – very important in a time of rigid class structures. Extra materials such as wire and lace were also used, again adding to the cost and making it harder for the lower classes to imitate. Ornamentation increased even more in the 1820s for much the same reasons. By the 1830s, puff sleeves had become so gargantuan that they needed supports to puff out properly, as well as plenty of servants to starch and clean them.

While this was an age of expansion for the middle classes, when men were able to amass their own fortunes based on their entrepreneurial skills, there was still only one option for women to secure wealth: the marriage market. Men used women's dresses to judge their class, helping them decide if it was worthwhile to approach them. The signs of wealth on early neoclassical styles were subtle, so the move towards extra ornamentation was a way of signposting a family's wealth to potential sons-in-law.

Bodices were a versatile and clever way of displaying gothic ornamentation, but with the added bonus that they could easily be transferred to other dresses, making them highly cost effective but glamorous at the same time! They were often ornate and made of expensive fabrics such as silk. They seem to have become popular during the 1810s, when ornate decoration started to become fashionable. Some were in the gothic style, with puffed, faux slashed sleeves and decoration; some featured heavy military-style braiding or button work. Instead of a new dress, women could buy a bodice as a cost-saving measure; wearing a fancier bodice over the top of a simple gown could give the same impression. These bodices were still used into the 1820s, even when the shape of dresses changed, with wider skirts and bigger sleeves.

GOTHIC BALLS

The Regency era saw a rise in the popularity of gothic balls, which offered a tantalising opportunity to become a gothic heroine for the night. Interest in medieval, Tudor and Stuart history became widespread: 'tragic' historical female figures such as Lady Jane Grey and Mary Queen of Scots featured widely in plays and at costume balls. These balls had a considerable influence on fashion; some costumes incorporated gauzy fabric and sequinned, metallic embellishments. Candlelight would give these historically influenced gowns a shimmering, ghostly or fae look. Some balls had stricter dress codes based on specific eras or dynasties, sometimes with the nobility dressing as their own ancestors! Accompanying books, fashion plates and even decorated fans were sold as mementos, in the same way commemorative fashion books and magazines are available today. Mainstream ballgowns soon followed suit, incorporating gothic hallmarks to add glamour to evening soirées.

Plays inspired by gothic novels were also widespread (copyright was not seen as an issue), sometimes becoming even more ghoulish than the books. Mary Shelley was delighted with the stage

Nostalgia could explain the growth of the gothic trend from novels to fashion, theatre and other areas of culture.

adaptation of *Frankenstein*, even though she didn't make a penny from it. Plays in particular allowed gothic trends to become accessible to even wider audiences, especially in the increasingly built-up urban areas. This helped gothic trends to trickle down to the working classes.

GOTHIC AND ROMANTIC

Nostalgia could explain the growth of the gothic trend from novels to fashion, theatre and other areas of culture, perhaps as part of a backlash against the Napoleonic Wars, the Industrial Revolution and rapidly advancing scientific progress. Science was often treated as theatre and played a sinister role in such gothic novels as *Frankenstein*. A terrible price already seemed to be being paid for scientific advances such as the Industrial Revolution, with the poor crammed into squalid conditions in the cities, reports of dead bodies on the streets and mortality rates climbing due to disease spreading more quickly in cramped living quarters.

In contrast to ever harsher reality, gothic books provided escapism while Romantic poetry celebrated the past – not with sensational horror stories, but by romanticising nature and simple country living.

Romantic ideas and the gothic, always hand-in-hand in the past, seemed to separate in the 1820s. While both styles continued to be historically influenced (by the 1820s it was the Tudors and Stuarts providing more inspiration than medieval), Romantic styles tended to be in paler shades and floral prints, while gothic styles were darker and more opulent.

Throughout the 1820s, floral patterned fabrics were incredibly popular. Embellishments such as frills, tabs and collars became commonplace on increasingly lengthy bodices. Sleeves were also generally 'gigot': puffed and long. Skirts also became wider, their construction changing from two panels to four, with hems becoming much heavier due to padding. The Romantic style obviously required much more fabric; ironically, by trying to celebrate the past and preserve a bygone era, wearers were funding a heavily industrialised future. A typical dress would have required on average about twelve yards of fabric, but, unlike the costly Indian muslins of the early 1800s, by 1830 most fabrics were made cheaply in British mills. Larger dresses with more ornamentation were now more easily affordable for more people, though at the cost of driving British cottage industries and overseas artisans out of business.

FANS

Handheld fans were a must-have fashion accessory for women for many centuries. They changed in accordance with taste in terms of size, shape, colour, design and material. Specific movements could be used

Portrait of Adriana Johanna van Wijck, Petrus van Schendel, 1829, Rijksmuseum. Adriana Johanna van Wijck is dressed in the Romantic style, with a dress made from patterned fabric, an ornate lace collar and double puffed sleeves – an inner and an outer layer, with the puffs the same size as her head.

Gothic revival fan, c.1820–1840, V&A.

to communicate secretly with friends and lovers, and they were the perfect way to accessorise any outfit.

In terms of materials used, mother-of-pearl (which could be dyed), ivory and tortoiseshell were at the expensive end of the market. Wood and cattle horn (which could be dyed to look like tortoiseshell) were cheaper.

In the early 1800s, fans were quite small, similarly as were dresses, probably as a reaction to the French Revolution and an attempt to show more reserve and less decadence. However, as the era progressed, fans become more extravagant and gothic.

Many late Regency fans resemble Tudor ruffs. There was also a trend for fans which looked like church spires; pointed at the top, 'à la cathédrale', they were very delicately engraved, like stained glass windows. To further display one's gothic leanings, examples of gothic buildings and scenes from gothic stories with people dressed in medieval or Renaissance costume could also be displayed on fans. Others would show scenes from myths or poetry.

Fan-making in Spain was big business, which perhaps explains the fashion for black lace fans. Black lace was often linked with Spanish women in the British imagination, thanks to the mantillas they wore to church. Mantillas and other veils featured heavily in gothic novels and were thus very desirable.

Brisé fan, 1800–1810, French,
Metropolitan Museum of Art.

WOMEN IN A CHANGING WORLD

To the modern eye, neoclassical styles look relatively demure, but they would be scorned by the Victorians for indecency. There are tales of girls wearing pink stockings or underskirts, or even dampening their clothes to make them look see-through. Cartoonists relished observing how little underwear, if any, was worn under neoclassical dresses. Only a set of stays, a single petticoat, stockings and perhaps a pair of drawers (though these were developed as the era progressed) would be required. Compared to the stays, corsets, layered petticoats and crinolines or panniers that came before and after, they could be quite scandalous.

Perhaps the reinforcing of the message that these styles made a woman look 'loose' played a role in the shift in fashion towards very conservative modes of dress by the 1820s.

In the 1810s, decorations on the lower skirt became popular, often involving extra embroidery, folds or flounces around the hem, giving the dress a more gothic look. This continued into the 1820s, when skirt decorations became increasingly padded, and the dresses were made from stiffer fabric, with more fragile flourishes. By 1830, skirts were much wider, and the fabric stiffer again. The padding also acted as part of the dress's structure, holding the A-line shape.

By the 1820s, dresses' necklines had crept up. Whereas, in the past, the appearance of a higher neckline could be achieved by wearing a chemise underneath, the dress itself now had a higher neck, allowing for the popular gothic flourishes of ruffs and vandyke collars.

The gothic and Romantic styles, at first merely fun fashion experiments, soon presented an opportunity to display wealth and enforce modesty because of the heavier nature of the styles. Ironically, when one considers the rebellious and alternative nature of today's gothic fashion, this process of romanticising the past actually helped to reinforce, rather than criticise, existing class structures and the subservient role of women in society.

It is often the case historically that periods of liberation are followed by periods of conservatism. This shift towards modesty in women's fashion echoed what was happening in other walks of life. When the Prince Regent became King George IV in 1820, both his and his wife Queen Caroline's scandalous extramarital exploits were common knowledge and frowned upon. Many liberals were keen to distance themselves from the ideals of the French Revolution, given how bloody the consequences had been. The resulting arrests and executions of not only the French royal family and nobility but also any of that country's liberal, intelligent elite who had initially backed the Revolution alarmed the British. As in the 1950s, and also in more recent years, the past was idealised, resulting in a revival of vintage styles against a backdrop of recession and political turmoil. Perhaps this is why entire wardrobes, rather than mere embellishments, began to be influenced by the past.

People turned to religion, especially the newer evangelical churches, for guidance, as they felt let down by the unpopular monarch, deflated by the dangers of revolution and exhausted from the long wars. Women, in particular, embraced these churches, as they provided more of a role for them in their communities, as pastors' or missionaries' wives. They hosted events, organised charities and become involved in politics on a major scale for the first time by creating church societies opposed to slavery. This came at the cost of having to be a perfect and modest Christian woman in all things, including modest dress.

Living in the cities gave middle- and upper-class women a desire to distance themselves from the unpleasantness of the slums, and the church provided a way to do this. This helped create the nineteenth-century ideal of different spheres for the sexes in the middle classes and above; the woman's place being safely in the home, with the church serving as a safe, respectable way to socialise and engage in charitable works. By the 1820s, exaggerated gothic and Romantic ornamentation could often give dresses a rather childish look, but this was at least safer – a childish woman was back in her place as the property of the family.

In the 1700s, men and women often socialised and discussed politics together. This would be phased out in the more propriety-conscious 1800s. The gothic novel, at first an escape route for upper- and middle-class women, became a self-parody, reinforcing the idea of women as damsels who needed protection. The stirrings of early feminism from the French Revolution and the likes of Mary Wollstonecraft were

quashed and grouped with the other supposed evils of lax Regency society.

Marrying together medieval, Tudor and Stuart styles, thicker fabric was used for gowns and bodices become longer and more embellished. Thicker fabrics and padded hemlines made the dresses sturdier, less transparent and generally more modest, celebrating a narrow waist, wide hips and a bust – the perfect childbearing figure – whereas previous fashions had, strangely, suited a more boyish figure while also celebrating sensuality by emphasising the bosom.

King William IV ascended the throne in 1830, and, along with Queen Adelaide, helped spearhead an increase in morality and propriety that would shape society for the rest of the century. Necklines were now high; full, floor-length skirts were made of thick, heavily printed fabric. When Auguste Racinet wrote his *Costume History* in 1888, he described how, in the early part of the nineteenth century, women danced about in 'all but transparent gauze' which left their 'attractions barely veiled'. His tone, and the salacious detail he supplied, shows he knew that this mode of dress would be considered disgraceful by his contemporaries. But gothic fashion was now the height of propriety for the rest of the nineteenth century.

MEN'S FASHION

At first glance, men's Regency fashion appears not to have been influenced by the gothic, but there were undertones. Its influence massively increased over the following two centuries, but some important

Trousers, a cutaway and a waistcoat
from 1833, Metropolitan Museum
of Art — all familiar to the three-
piece suits men wear today. The
simpler waistcoats worn during the
Regency are very similar to modern
waistcoats, whereas in previous
centuries, they covered the thighs.

Riding boots (as worn by George Harley Drummond and painted by Henry Raeburn in 1808–9, Metropolitan Museum of Art); along with their obvious practical use, they became an essential component of a gentleman's informal wardrobe during this period.

hallmarks were introduced at this time, such as the modern suit (and trousers!). As well as setting standards for mainstream men's fashion, many of the archetypes associated with male gothic fashion stem from the Regency.

As with women's fashion, the French Revolution also had a sobering effect on men's fashion, from the made-up peacocks (known as 'macaronis') of the 1700s, to the simple, sleek (yet still expensive) understated fashion favoured by the likes of Beau Brummel, with fitted breeches, waistcoats and cutaways (forerunners to tailcoats). Less was more.

Tailcoats are still both a staple for formal menswear and also very much part of gothic fashion for both men and women. Black riding boots were increasingly worn, not only by soldiers but also by men partaking in the newly fashionable pursuits of walking and riding that encouraged a more athletic physique. No modern goth would be without a pair of big black boots.

The French Revolution wasn't the only factor in the more toned-down appearance of men's fashions. During the Napoleonic Wars, many young men became soldiers and wore their dress uniforms to fashionable balls and parties. The fitted jackets and trousers of their military uniforms influenced men's fashion of the day, and even young men who weren't soldiers would undoubtedly want to ensure they still looked manly and athletic. To achieve this, some even wore corsets and girdles under their clothes. Crisp, clean, high collars also provided a serious and sharp

A man's shirt from 1816–17, Metropolitan Museum of Art, with a high neck and a white ruffle. It would not look out of place today in a modern goth shop.

A man's shirt from 1816–17, Metropolitan Museum of Art, with a high neck and a white ruffle. It would not look out of place today in a modern goth shop.

masculine look and could be made even more rigid by the use of starch and the addition of stocks (see image right).

The rage for Greek and Roman statues made young, muscular men the height of fashion – perhaps one of the few times in history when the idealised male form received as much attention as the female. Tight breeches in buff or fawn, as near to flesh colour as possible, could indeed be likened to a nude leg. Trousers were generally worn for walking and other countryside pursuits, but gradually made their way into formal fashion throughout the era as the look of an active country gent became *de rigueur* – for some, this might also have added some gothic cachet, conjuring images of striding about windswept moors. The flesh-coloured tightly fitted breeches of the era could be likened to the hose or tights worn by medieval and Renaissance men, so even this very dandyish fashion was inspired by the historical flavour in the air.

The Industrial Revolution was another factor; it became more respectable for gentlemen to be actively employed due to the rise of the middle classes. For this, they needed a dark and serious wardrobe – hence the development of the three-piece suit (which was conceived in the 1600s but only really started to take shape as we know it in this era). Men's fashion has never really recovered from this time – often known as the Great Masculine Renunciation – when bright colours and impracticality were rejected.

While wearing greens, greys and blues mixed with browns and fawns was common, all black became more popular. It still held gothic undertones, however – still being associated with mourning, the clergy and the sinister figures of gothic novels. Black also had the added advantage of making the wearer look serious and gloomy, very desirable in the days of Romantic poetry and gothic fiction. Gothic style icons emerged during this era, including Lord Byron with his tousled cravats, dark hair and cloaks. The gentleman vampire, the inspiration for Dracula and many a gothic male ever since, emerged from John William Polidori's *The Vampyre*, which was inspired by Byron. This was the beginning of the classic sinister, noble, mysterious vampire, found not only in the figure of Count Dracula but also in many other gothic heroes.

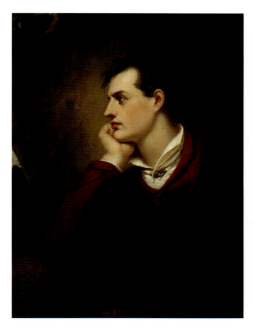

George Gordon Byron, 6th Baron Byron, Richard Westall, 1812.

Portrait of Percy Bysshe Shelley, Amelia Ciuran, 1819.

Bryon was a scandalous trensetter in his time, rather like a modern rock star, and many a young man tried to emulate his look and lifestyle. Bad-boy poets were icons, and what can be more gothic than that? As well as Polidori, Byron was also friends with the Romantic poet Percy Bysshe Shelley. Shelley's wife Mary, writer of *Frankenstein* and daughter of feminist Mary Wollstonecraft, was also stepsister to Claire Clairmont, one of Byron's mistresses. When her husband drowned, Mary Shelley, in a suitably gothic gesture, kept his mummified heart.

Greatcoats were very fashionable for men of all classes, worn by coach drivers and gentlemen alike. This added to their air of mystery. (Who *is* that man?)

They were a combination of a cape (in reference to Renaissance fashion) and a cloak (fashionable at the beginning of the Regency era), in the form of a coat. Large collars which could be flipped up and shoulder-length capes were useful for protecting the wearer from the elements when riding, with the added bonus of obscuring the face and figure, perfect for lurking on dark nights. The long coats were also perfect for keeping pristine outfits dry and clean, and for dramatically sweeping in and out of rooms! More practical than the cloaks they were descended from, they covered the body more closely and securely and provided more warmth. Long black coats are still a vital part of the gothic look today.

Increasingly, gothic ornamentation became an important way to show off a family's wealth.

John Hetherington is credited with inventing the tall, cylindrical top hat in 1797. It caused quite a stir when it premiered, and Hetherington was arrested for a breach of the peace! Ironically, it soon became a symbol of the establishment it had initially shocked. Tall, often dark and always dramatic, the top hat has remained a staple of formal men's attire, adopted by modern-day goths of both genders. Like a cloak or a corset, it is a blatantly obvious reference to fashions of the past. As well as conjuring an image of a gentleman of bygone days, the top hat bears a resemblance to other historical hats, most notably those worn by Puritans in the 1600s, which influenced and morphed into the stereotypical tall witch's and wizard's hats we see in countless representations today.

CONCLUSION

Perhaps it was only natural that, after the simplicity of neoclassical gowns inspired by the ancient world, fashion should move to the drama of gothic fashion, inspired by the medieval, Tudor and Stuart eras. Interests in these historic periods also matched the changing mood of the Regency period; new, liberal regimes were looking to the democracies of the ancient world, while British dynasties of the past were looked at for inspiration, at a time when the reality of living in a modernising world seemed more frightening than thrilling.

The first three decades of the nineteenth century followed a period of tumultuous uprisings and change; due to the upper class's keenness to preserve the social structure, they saw a gradual tightening of social codes. Gothic (and Romantic fashion) provided a way of looking back at the past with rose-tinted spectacles – the good old days of damsels in distress.

Increasingly, gothic ornamentation became an important way to show off a family's wealth. As women – seen as the property of their family – were more likely to be wearing the ornamentation, they also became models for their family's respectability.

The towns that grew during the Industrial Revolution threw people closer together; for the middle classes and above, this provided more of an excuse to attend gatherings and show off their wealth through fashion – so, the showier, the better. However, the realities of industrialisation, combined with the aftermath of revolution and war, seemed too much, too harsh and too soon. While many benefited from modernisations in industry and science, the middle and upper classes had no desire to be faced with unsightly factories and the misery of the urban poor, and they took refuge, literally, in their increasingly respectable homes and families, as well as figuratively in the idealisation of bygone ages. The resulting reversion to conservative social behaviours seemed a good compromise to many. It can be

A View in the Pantheon, London, Winter fashions, 1834–1835, V&A. Fashions of the 1830s were a lot more obviously gothic, with darker colours, long coats, top hats, small waists and big skirts. As well as drawing on Elizabethan fashion, this decade and those which followed would set the trends for future gothic movements.

argued, therefore, that fear and panic at the advent of a modern age created the shift in fashion towards historically inspired gothic.

While the Regency may not seem like a remotely gothic era to the casual observer, I hope this chapter has illustrated how a gothic undercurrent lay beneath fashion and popular culture, slowly developing through the novels, art and mood of the era, until

what we consider gothic took root. The Regency goths were the first to consciously choose to dress in a historically and imaginatively inspired way, in contrast to the mainstream fashions of their time. It seems a shame that in the later Regency period these fun, imaginative fashions were used as tools for a more conservative society; but the story of goths was only just beginning...

1830s-1901

Victorian Gothic

W ith the coronation of Queen Victoria in 1838, the Victorian age officially began. A well-behaved young queen who quickly became a wife and a mother set the tone for an era that idealised wifely devotion.

As much as Victoria's adoration for her beloved Prince Albert was a model for the first part of her reign, her extravagant mourning, lasting for decades after his death, heavily influenced for the middle and later part of her reign, giving much of the nineteenth century a decidedly gothic tone. After Prince Albert's death in 1861, mourning practices became more regimented and fashionable than ever, meaning that gothic looks helped define the era.

Many of the hallmarks of the modern goth look either originated or were popular in this era, including long skirts, corsets, crinolines, capes, top hats, tailcoats and great coats.

In popular culture, gothic fiction remained in high demand. The Aesthetic Movement grew in popularity

Bridge of Sighs (1858) by Sir John Everett Millais, Art Institute of Chicago, showing a woman wearing a long cloak and skirts.

Modern re-imagining of a Victorian
widow wearing a veil.

Woman in a red-off the shoulder Victorian influenced gown.

towards the end of the century, as artists such as the Pre-Raphaelites looked to the past, especially the medieval period, for inspiration, mimicking fashion as well as art.

The leaps and bounds made by the Industrial Revolution heralded the beginnings of faster, cheaper, mass-produced fashion, meaning that fashionable experimentation became more accessible to more people. There were other changes in the way clothes were made, such as the invention of boldly coloured chemical dyes. The fashionable lifespan of an item was shortened, as new trends were rapidly churned out to replace the old.

In women's fashion, a small waist and a full skirt was the order of the Victorian era, in complete contrast to the Regency. The Romantic and gothic bell-shaped skirts of the 1830s remained in fashion for decades. The width of the skirt built up to its peak in the 1860s, before slimming back down again, but not before a craze for excessive volume at the back of the gown – but more on that later.

Men's fashion continued down the sombre path it had embarked on in the Regency. Dark formal attire was often worn on a day-to-day basis, contrasting with colourful, patterned womenswear.

The exception to this was mourning wear, which was worn by both sexes but more noticeable on women, as they tended to wear it for longer periods. Ordinarily, upper- and middle-class women would not wear black at any other time. Since the Victorian obsession with mourning garb has had such a profound influence on not only how we view nineteenth-century fashion but also on many a young goth's idealised version of gothic fashion, it seems only right to begin by examining it.

The corseted waist of Annie Louise Ames (c.1885).

Queen Victoria, the Crown Princess of Prussia, Princess Alice and Prince Alfred in mourning, William Bambridge, 1862.

MOURNING

Many of our ideas about historical mourning date from the Victorian period, and, likewise, many ideals of Victorian dress conjure images of crepe, veils and black gowns. Mourning is synonymous with the period.

As with the Regency, class boundaries were increasingly important to the Victorians, due to the growth of the middle classes brought about by the Industrial Revolution and the expansion of the British Empire. Having a society with strict social codes and norms may seem baffling and inaccessible to us, but that was the point. Advancement in society was a game you won by knowing all the rules and displaying to everyone else how well you understood them. Mourning was one way to do this.

With mourning, as with many things Victorian, there was an element of 'keeping up with the Joneses'. Wearing black represented your inner sadness; there are stories of people competing with neighbours or friends to outdo each other in their displays of grief and prove who had loved the best. Men often wrapped crepe around their top hats; once, two widowers in the same town gradually increased the crepe on their hats until it became bigger than the headwear itself.

This sounds rather a cynical view of mourning dress, but there was also a practical and compassionate reason for it. Dressing in mourning told everyone

around you that you were coping with a loss, almost like 'a handle with care sign'. Childhood mortality was still high in the Victorian period, and life expectancy was between forty and fifty. Due to the nature of many infectious diseases, such as cholera, which raged during this time, you could be healthy one day and dead the next, leaving friends and families rocked by shock and grief – having a way to communicate this was helpful. More people than ever before had

Lady in Mourning, Hildegard Thorell, 1896, Nationalmuseum.

moved into large, impersonal cities, and, whereas their forebears may have lived in villages where everybody knew each other's business, visual social cues become more important when interacting with strangers.

One wasn't expected to wear black for years for every passing acquaintance; etiquette governed who should wear what and for how long, depending on who had died. There were also different stages of mourning, such as full and half mourning. Full mourning required the wearing of black, plain clothes in heavy non-reflective materials such as crepe, poplin and bombazine, and the avoidance of shiny jewellery such as jade. A mourner's grief was expected to be so powerful that there would have been no time for thoughts of personal vanity.

During half mourning, rules were eased, allowing a choice of fabrics as well as greys and purples. It was also thought to be in bad taste to immediately revert to bright colours, even if appropriate mourning times had been observed.

Women observed mourning more closely and for longer periods than men. This was the case for all relations, but especially for spouses. It was more socially acceptable for a widowers to remarry quickly after the death of his wife (often to have someone to look after the house and children) than for a widow. Victorians idealised the dutiful wife; what better way to show your devotion to your husband than to mourn him for a longer period?

In certain circumstances, widows could inherit money and property, meaning that being a widow was, arguably, the most powerful position a woman could hold: she was not as beholden to her parents as an unmarried woman, but as soon as she remarried, all her property would be transferred to her new husband. Widows' weeds could, therefore, be seen as a symbol of power and independence.

A widow was expected to wear full mourning for a year and then half mourning for another year; even darker underclothes were available for women. On the other hand, widowers only wore mourning for a year. They wore black suits, neckties and gloves with black crepe wrapped around their hats. Black armbands were commonly seen on men whose job required a non-black uniform, or who were too poor to afford a new black suit. Black tie pins, cufflinks and black-edged linen were also worn. Whilst everyday Victorian menswear was generally sombre and dark, it would have been a clear signal of mourning to wear an entirely black outfit. Men and women in the same household tended to coordinate their mourning wear – if the women weren't in mourning, neither were the men.

In general, parents wore mourning for a year after the death of a child, as did adults mourning their parents (contrary to many modern portrayals, young children were not expected to wear mourning – although, some did). A six-month mourning period was expected for the deaths of siblings and grandparents; it was two months for aunts and uncles, six weeks for great-aunts and great-uncles and a month for first cousins. Since these were only guidelines, some mourned for longer. Those who mourned for a shorter

Mourning broaches, 1860s,
Metropolitan Museum of Art.

time might provoke disapproval, but it was allowed.

After Prince Albert's death, mourning became so rigid and widespread that there were specialist mourning department stores and warehouses, as well as a 'cult of death', with professional mourners and elaborate funerals.

'Memento moris' (Latin for 'Remember you must die') were personal mementos and keepsakes commemorating the dead, including jewellery (often made from jet), as well as pictures of the dead, engravings about mortality and motifs of skulls and bones on items such as clocks or gravestones.

Photographs of dead bodies were commonplace; seen today as a hallmark of horror films, they were a thoughtful way to remember the dead. As photography was relatively new, people were still not photographed widely, perhaps only for special occasions. The ability to capture an image of a loved one so perfectly (perhaps the only one that existed) before they were buried must have been very powerful. It was a growing industry, and some photographers even employed people to touch up the images by painting the eyes to make them appear open, as if the sitter were still alive.

Jewellery to commemorate the deceased often included hair: For the rest of her life, Queen Victoria

wore a locket containing a lock of Prince Albert's hair. Victorians also wore jewellery such as brooches and necklaces using hair as their entire base material. They also wove wreaths and decorated their houses with it. In the early twentieth century, changing ideas about cleanliness saw this style change.

As well as mourning wear for all the family, mourning accessories were needed for the home. It was easier to buy all one's mourning goods under one roof, meaning that mourning warehouses became one of the first types of department stores. The first to open was Jay's of Regent Street, offering clothes and any other mourning accoutrements that might be needed. The business model of such stores was shrewd, as to wear mourning clothes for another death or to keep them in the house when the mourning period was finished was considered bad luck.

Jay's opened in 1841, showing that large-scale, extravagant mourning was becoming commonplace even before Prince Albert's death; however, Queen Victoria took these already established nineteenth-century norms and ran with them, amplifying and popularising the practice. She was in full mourning for three years (longer than guidelines suggested), and then continued in various other stages of mourning for the rest of her life: another forty years.

Mourning was spread throughout classes but easier to follow if you were rich; you would be expected to purchase a whole new mourning wardrobe, not to be worn at any other time. To avoid bad luck, mourning clothes were often sold or given away after the required period had ended. The Victorian era saw a boom in the second-hand clothing market; clothes became cheaper due to more efficient production methods, so the wealthy refreshed their wardrobes at a faster rate than ever before.

Servants were often given mourning clothes, particularly if their employers were wealthy. (It is worth remembering that people across the middle-class spectrum would have had servants of some description, given the lengthy nature of household tasks before the invention of electronic gadgets.) In less affluent households, servants would only don black armbands.

Mourning clothes could be rented for funerals, allowing families to at least put on a show for a day, although working-class clothes tended to be darker and more hard-wearing, anyway. People could also hire mourners to pad out the crowd if they thought a funeral would be poorly attended. If mourning clothes were impossible due to lack of time or money, then darker everyday clothes were considered acceptable.

While these lists of rules and customs may seem confusing, there was help at hand from many journals, magazines and books about the correct ways to mourn, including such well-known publications as *The Queen* and *Cassell*.

Victorian graveyards are iconic, especially the so-called 'Magnificent Seven' in London (including Highgate, which is linked to vampire stories). The Père Lachaise cemetery in Paris is famous for its ornate graves and the famous people buried there. Elaborate burial places were a way of displaying both grief and wealth at a time when mortality rates were relatively high and affected all walks of life. They weren't just a fashion trend, however: increased migration into the cities through the eighteenth and nineteenth centuries created a need for large public burial spaces.

Another reason for elaborate graves was the fear of grave robbers. The so-called 'resurrection men' stole bodies to be used in surgeons' experiments, and they posed a very real threat. Gates, vaults and mausoleums were a lot harder to break into than simple graves. To deter grave robbers, guards would be posted over family graves for the first few nights while the body was still fresh; sometimes a bell was installed, attached with a rope to the dead person's hand in case they had accidently been buried alive.

Cemeteries were designed to be beautiful and welcoming. People would take day trips to visit them and have tours and picnics. (This still happens today, most stereotypically with goths, but some of the more famous cemeteries do hold tours, such as the Saint Louis cemetery in New Orleans; some even have licences to allow marriage services, such as Arnos Vale in Bristol.) Famously, on the Mexican Day of the Dead, locals gather around the graves of their loved ones with decorations and food, bringing a festive

Widow with Ennui (1868) by James Jacques Joseph Tissot. For some, prolonged periods of mourning were something of a chore, confined as they were to dark clothes and sedate activities.

atmosphere to Mexican graveyards. In the Victorian period, as now, they were a good place to hold clandestine meetings, with lots of stone structures to hide behind. Percy and Mary Shelley used to meet in the cemetery of St Pancras Old Church, at the grave of Mary's mother, Mary Wollstonecraft.

Many families saved up to make funerals extravagant spectacles. Women often did not attend, as it was considered impolite, although this changed depending on the era and social class. Some women made their own shrouds and included them in their trousseaux when they got married.

Other rules for how to behave went further than how to dress and decorate your home. If you were

in deep mourning, you were not allowed to go into society for up to six months (for example, to balls, the theatre or assemblies, although some reports suggest concerts were exempt). It seems that discretion could be exercised (provided that the entertainments attended were not too rambunctious) depending on circumstances and the temperament of the mourner, as even some Victorians appreciated that prolonged isolation in grief was not good for one's mental health.

We often think of Victorians as being obsessed with death, but they were simply marking it in elaborate ways. Despite the Victorians' supposed inhibitions, a lengthy grieving period did provide time and space for discussions about loss and grief.

MAGIC, THE SUPERNATURAL AND PERFORMANCE

Even though the Victorians lived through a time of great scientific advancement, they were superstitious and religious. With the rapid rise of new technologies, the lines between magic and technology became blurred, and ideas about what could be achieved, witnessed and experienced seemed limitless. Many people looked for ways to connect with the 'other side', whether that be deceased loved ones or fairies. People looking for answers were willing to try a wide range of techniques and specialisms, including séances, spiritualism, mesmerism, hypnosis and the use of mediums.

Séances were often very theatrical. As well as channelling the voices of the dead, furniture would sometimes move or imprints would be left on malleable substances such as hot wax. Even Queen Victoria visited a medium to try to receive messages from Prince Albert once he had passed on.

Male mediums were often reviled, as it was seen as an exclusively feminine craft; women were thought to be more delicate and therefore more susceptible to influences from beyond the grave. Female mediums would often attend on grieving households, so wearing black apparel and a veil would have been very fitting. Mediums were often portrayed as gypsy women, travellers who lived outside of society, dressed in folk costume often involving layered skirts, jangling jewellery, scarves, bodices and bells. They were a little like Victorian witches.

Page from an album of spirit photographs, Frederick Hudson, 1872, Metropolitan Museum of Art.

Modern gothic interpretations of the Victorian circus style. The Victorian circus costumes allowed more flesh to be revealed than was respectable in everyday dress. So-called 'tattooed ladies' (as well as men) worked as attractions in circuses or freak shows.

Circuses, freak shows and stage magicians toured the country, performing in big tops and theatres. Due to the peripatetic nature of their industry and the lengths they went to maintain their stage secrets, they were treated with both admiration and suspicion. The darker side and cruelty of the business were never far from the surface, meaning that Victorian circuses and performers, as well as mediums and fortune tellers, are very much alive in the gothic imagination, often featuring in modern horror films. Their exaggerated, sexy and dramatic versions of nineteenth-century dress and folk costumes are very inspiring to gothic fashionistas.

Interest in the occult grew, in general, and magical organisations such as the Golden Dawn were established. While this did not become mainstream, the witch hunts of old had been relegated to history, so dabbling with and discussing magical practices and spell work did not come with the threat of torture and death.

Science seemed like magic to some people, so while it seems strange that these practices were popular within reserved Victorian society, it is important to remember that science was changing at such a rapid pace that anything seemed possible.

GOTHIC FICTION IN THE NINETEENTH CENTURY

During the nineteenth century, gothic fiction came of age. At the beginning of the century, it was a publishing sensation but rapidly became a clichéd parody of itself as it reached the mass market. It had many offshoots, such as horror stories, science fiction, penny dreadfuls and detective stories, as well as casting a heavy shadow over the mainstream and even literary fiction of its day. The end of the century culminated rather satisfyingly with the publication of Bram Stoker's *Dracula*.

Features of gothic fiction included transporting the reader to a different time, either involving historical settings, ghosts and immortals, or both. This reflected an uneasiness many Victorians felt with their fast-changing, technologically evolving world and the struggle between the mythology and beliefs of old Europe and the unbelievable, almost magical scientific discoveries of the new age.

Young women in danger is a well-known trope of the genre – it is safer to read about these things than experience them. The examinations of power and

Cover of *Varney the Vampire*.

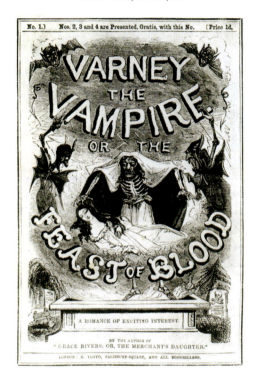

sexual undertones featured in much gothic literature may have been alarming for prudish Victorian society, but were undoubtedly appealing, as shown by the popularity of such books. A juxtaposition between the virtuous woman and the new, increasingly feminist woman or the so-called 'fallen' woman (such as Lucy and Mina in *Dracula*) was one way of looking at this.

After Polidori used Lord Bryon as his inspiration for the gentlemanly eponymous character in *The Vampyre*, other authors followed his lead. *Varney the Vampire* was a popular series of cheap penny-dreadful pamphlets published in the middle of the century, featuring the terrifyingly undead Lord Varney. Sheridan Le Fanu's short story *Carmilla* introduced a vampire as a female seductress. The growing trend for beautiful, sophisticated blood suckers crossed over into art. In 1897, the same year *Dracula* was released, Philip Burne-Jones painted *The Vampire*, featuring a thin woman in a white robe with long dark hair.

Changing shape or becoming monstrous was something Victorian gothic fiction really embraced, with classics such as *Jekyll and Hyde* and *Dracula*. The preoccupation with shape-shifting monsters possibly stems from Charles Darwin's *On the Origin of Species* in 1859, with its shocking discussions about human evolution, as well as the discoveries and identifications of dinosaur bones by people like Mary Anning (1799–1847). The Victorian obsession with respectability was an additional factor.

Jekyll and Hyde was inspired by the real-life Dr Hunter, for whom resurrectionists (grave robbers)

Changing shape or becoming monstrous was something Victorian gothic fiction really embraced.

provided corpses for experiments in his own house. The veneer of Victorian respectability was threatened by ideas embedded in gothic fiction: Oscar Wilde's *The Picture of Dorian Gray* plays on fears that something sinister lurks behind a smart appearance. As does *Jekyll and Hyde*, published shortly before Jack the Ripper began his murderous spree, and which became linked with these crimes in the public's imagination – so much so that when *Jekyll and Hyde* was made into a stage show, the actor who played them, Richard Mansfield, was even accused of being Jack the Ripper!

Although he has now fallen into obscurity, George W.M. Reynolds once outsold Charles Dickens. He wrote *Wagner, the Wehr-Wolf* in 1847, considered one of the first English-language novels to feature a werewolf. Werewold mythology was much more prevalent in medieval and Renaissance Europe, where wolves survived and lived in greater numbers than in Britain. There were even some instances of people being tried as werewolves, in a similar way to witch trials.

Gothic fiction casts such a spectre over the century that it makes its way into many of the iconic texts of the era, for example, Emily Brontë's *Wuthering Heights*. This all helps to add to the mood and zeitgeist of the era, not only influencing how people thought and acted at the time but also how we view and idealise the era today. It is one of the reasons why modern goths emulate Victorian dress: so many gothic stories date from this period. This was also the century when blood-sucking figures from folklore became more refined into the characters we know today as vampires – undead beings synonymous with nobility and style.

Penny bloods, which later became penny dreadfuls, started life in the 1830s, at a time when literacy levels were increasing across classes and faster printing presses could meet the increased demand for cheaper reading material. The books initially featured sensational tales of pirates and highwaymen and were often serialised. They also tended to feature gothic traits: strange places (i.e. prisons and moors), virginal damsels in distress and dark themes. The popularity of these books exposed more people to gothic ideas, stories and conventions. They were gory, melodramatic and filled with death and violence. By the 1860s, tastes had moved on from highwaymen and pirates to detectives. The development of the modern police force changed society and fiction forever.

Wilkie Collins and Edgar Allan Poe both pioneered early detective and mystery novels, known at the time as sensation novels; they featured gothic settings and elements, along with some sort of perilous mystery. The poet Charles Baudelaire, who translated Poe's work into French, had some very gothic credentials of his own. As well as writing a poem about a rotting corpse, he was also known for mostly dressing in black in mourning for the death of Romanticism, and for dyeing his hair green.

Even Charles Dickens dabbled in the gothic; many of his works include gothic elements, such as the ghosts in *A Christmas Carol*, the deaths (including a spontaneous human combustion) and vulnerable

Miss Havisham, played by Helena
Bonham Carter in a BBC production of
Great Expectations, 2012, BBC Films.

young women in *Bleak House*, as well as orphans aplenty from Pip in *Great Expectations* to Oliver Twist. *Great Expectations* encompasses many gothic traits, including the mystery around Pip's inheritance along with his encounter with Magwitch in the graveyard and the multiple deaths, while the gothic archetype of the jilted bride is personified in Miss Havisham, almost an amalgamation of a ghost and a witch.

Dickens was not the first to portray a tragically jilted bride – they had been a staple of ghost stories for centuries – but Miss Havisham certainly became the benchmark. Her hold on the public imagination may partly stem from the idea of the white wedding dress worn only once, something that only really took hold in the Victorian era thanks to Queen Victoria's choice of wedding gown. Before this, the bride commonly wore a new or favourite dress which was often worn again. Ghostly brides, in torn or aged wedding gowns, are a staple of modern Halloween costumes; fa famous modern example is Tim Burton's *Corpse Bride*. The tragic bride trope encapsulates the ideal of a gothic novel: beauty, youth, promise and hope has been lost or threatened, and turned by tragedy and fate into something repulsive and frightening. (To the average Victorian woman, the idea of being jilted was even more terrifying than it is today, as any hope of a stable future was tied up in a secure marriage.)

Whereas in other eras (such as the Regency and the twentieth century) people dressed to emulate characters in gothic fiction, in Victorian times it became such a popular genre that it seeped into mainstream fiction and often had contemporary settings – the threat of horror impinging on people's everyday lives. In terms of fashion, the Victorian era inspired twentieth-century goths, in the same way that the medieval era inspired Regency gothic.

TARTAN

Tartan had been outlawed in the early eighteenth century in an attempt to quell Scottish nationalism. However, on Queen Victoria's visit to Scotland in 1842, many Scottish traditions were revived for the enchanted queen (presumably the powers that be had decided that all the nationalism had been quelled in Scotland for the time being). The fashion-conscious queen responded by enthusiastically wearing tartan. Tartan gowns become popular, as did trousers and waistcoats, and it was used in trims for accessories such as bonnets. This was the first time tartan was widely worn as part of mainstream fashion throughout the whole of the British Isles.

A tartan waistcoat or vest from the
1850s, Metropolitan Museum of Art.

Tartan still has fashion appeal today and is associated with goth's fashion cousin, punk. It's frequently used by designers with a gothic, punky aesthetic, most famously by Vivienne Westwood, who works with Harris tweed, and by Alexander McQueen, most notably in his *Highland Rape* collection. Tartan evokes strong ideals of heritage and history, appealing to fans of the gothic aesthetic, and, of course, it goes well with black – some tartans, such as the green and black of the Black Watch regiment, use particularly dark colour combinations. The wearing of a kilt also can be seen as an act of rebellion, since it was an outlawed garment. It is also one of the few British folk costumes that have survived from ancient times, giving it even more mysterious appeal.

VICTORIAN MAKE-UP

Tanned skin only became fashionable in twentieth-century British society. Before that, pale skin was highly favoured. As well as proving you didn't work on the land, as mentioned earlier, there are also racial connotations: pure white skin was presumed to display your supposedly pure northern European heritage.

The Tudors and Georgians powdered and painted their faces white, even using poisonous substances such as lead to achieve the desired whiter-than-white look. In the Victorian period, natural beauty was prized and wearing obvious make-up was looked down on; it was still used,

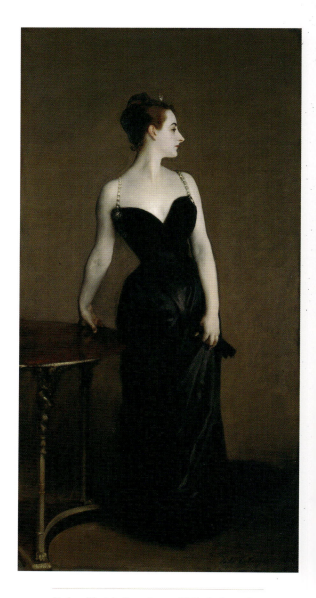

Madame X by John Singer Sargent (1883–4), Metropolitan Museum of Art, depicts Madame Pierre Gautreau in a surprisingly revealing dress for the 1880s, showing off her ghostly white skin.

1840s fashion plate, French, Rijksmuseum.

but covertly. It was generally used to subtly enhance existing features, for example, making cheeks and lips slightly redder, and was often made with more natural ingredients.

The exception to this was enamelling, which entailed having the face and sometimes the neck painted white, lasting for a few weeks. This paint was so thick it covered lines in the skin. It is thought to have been used mostly by rich older women, as well as prostitutes and stage performers. The middle class, desperate for respectability, would never have admitted to using it, and it was generally ridiculed. It produced almost ghost-white skin (some would even paint faint veins over the white to give the impression of even paler skin). Recipes for the enamel paste varied; lead was probably no longer used by this time, but as it was such a covert practice, we cannot be entirely sure.

Modern goths are known for painting their skin white, inspired in part by these old fashion beauty ideals, as well as by its supernatural connotations.

DECADE BY DECADE

The differences between early and late Victorian fashion, especially women's fashion, are quite marked. Each decade has influenced gothic fashion in some way. Moving through the decades from the beginning to the end of Victoria's reign, we can see how fashion shifted and how the gothic imagination lingered. It is not so much that Victorian fashion was consciously gothic, but how Victorian fashions have influenced the gothic ever since.

1840s

The 1840s saw the further development of Romantic and gothic fashions from the 1820s and 1830s. They matured and became less childish in appearance. While sleeves were still puffed, they were no longer bigger than the wearer's head. Flounces and other decorative touches became more toned down and skirts became wider and longer than the dresses of the 1820s, covering ankles and feet. Hairstyles also became much less extravagant, while floral patterns continued to grow in popularity and became the mainstay.

White dresses, in favour for over thirty years, were no longer fashionable for everyday wear, and took on marital connotations after Queen Victoria wore white for her love-matched royal wedding to Prince Albert. Royal brides had worn silver before this. Queen Victoria's wedding in 1840 was one of the first to be widely read about in magazines and newspapers, and, as a pretty young bride and a handsome groom, they unknowingly set the template for Western weddings for the next two centuries.

Queen Victoria and Prince Albert were also advocates of traditional family life; even though she was a queen and empress, the couple cultivated the image of a traditional husband and wife with a large family. This was a welcome change from the partying excesses of the late Georgian monarchs, but liberal ideals stagnated under the resulting return to conservatism. Styles became more modest to reflect the modes of the time, but the young queen still liked fashion, however, so big ball gowns, coloured florals and pretty bonnets reigned – as long as too much flesh wasn't revealed!

A more conservative woman was the archetype of Victorian femininity, and however beautiful their clothes were, they reached new depths of restrictive impracticality, with very long skirts supported by layers of heavy petticoats. (The crinoline, a surprisingly practical garment, was yet to be invented, so bell-shaped skirts were fabricated using multiple layers.) Some women wore up to seven petticoats, although two was most common, stiffness and volume being achieved by making the petticoats out of horsehair. Protruding petticoat frills and puff ball tulle skirts are a favourite with goths thanks to fashions like these.

The ideal look for an 1840s woman was a long-sleeved fitted top and a bell-shaped, floor-length skirt. The high waist of the Regency was gone; they were now more in line with the natural waist, allowing for longer bodices. Corsets covered the torso from below the waist to over the bust. They were laced at the back, especially for wealthy women. There tended to be a long pocket or channel between the breasts where the busk could be inserted, a long, flat piece of wood, metal or bone which flattened the stomach.

Many Victorian corsets employed steel, whereas other more flexible materials had been used previously; Regency stays had been much less restrictive. Small waists were fashionable in the 1840s, so tight lacing was the order of the day – although probably not quite as tight as we are led to believe. Some photographs showing extremely small waists have been doctored. Unlike many modern goths influenced by this period, corsets were not displayed over other garments but were hidden and functioned as underwear.

The 1840s were extremely conservative, so a woman's body was almost completely covered; even the face was obscured by a bonnet, especially in daywear fashions and when leaving the house. A lady was never without her gloves, and capes were used to

1840s fashion plate, French, Rijksmuseum.

Modes de Vienne et de Paris.

of gowns from the 1660s, which, although it had been a very loose and licentious period, was considered acceptable, as it celebrated the Restoration of the Stuart Monarchy. Ironically, it was therefore seen in a positive light by the more conservative Victorians, with the British monarchy having been restored in 1660 after a failed experiment with republicanism.

Aside from the collars of ballgowns, trim and excessive detailing was not widespread. Dresses tended to be simpler, with detachable collars and cuffs of lace or similar fabric which could be swapped between dresses. Fabrics were often patterned in florals or plaid and came in various colours. Silk became more widespread in day gowns. In another nod to the past, it became fashionable to recycle silk from eighteenth-century dresses to make new ones; the pastel colours and florals patterns were of a similar taste, and the amount of fabric required was similar.

Mantles, capes and shawls were very popular, a motif which still features in gothic fashion today, as well as harking back to Regency veils, often used to denote the gothic when referencing medieval and other bygone eras. It was not considered polite in the 1840s for a woman to appear outside without an additional covering over her dress.

Inspired by Queen Victoria's wedding attire, it became very fashionable to wear artificial flowers in one's hair, although thanks to the use of arsenic to produce the colour green, working conditions were appalling and sometimes fatal for the girls involved in their manufacture.

cover the long skirts when coats and jackets wouldn't stretch that far. The puffed sleeves had deflated somewhat; they were more practical and gave a demure and modest look.

Ballgowns were allowed to reveal a little more flesh than daywear, being off the shoulder and short-sleeved. They were wide and heavily trimmed, so, in fact, not particularly revealing at all. They mimicked the styles

Menswear

Dark fitted suits were the order of the day, with the aim being to achieve a look of refined middle-class respectability. Men's clothes of the 1830s had been somewhat exaggerated, with padded shoulders and small waists, but 1840s suits had a more natural look. Dark-coloured frock coats were fashionable daywear in this period – and are still a desirable item in any modern gothic wardrobe. By the end of the decade, they featured increasingly in evening wear.

The long fitted trousers, normally in plaid or grey, did not tend to match the waistcoats and jackets, and allowed a little variation in the otherwise serious ensemble. Collars were still starched and upturned and matched with cravats or dark ties – all still seen in gothic wear today. The top hat was a ubiquitous part of men's fashion, tending to be black and about seven inches tall. They were often made from beaver fur, and hatters suffered the occupational hazard of going mad thanks to the use of mercury in the production process, hence the 'Mad Hatter' in Lewis Carroll's *Alice's Adventures in Wonderland*.

1850s

This decade saw the peak of bell-shaped skirts as crinolines were developed. Wide-supported skirts had been fashionable in the Tudor period, with support in the form of cylindrical farthingales, and in the Georgian period, when they had been supported by wide, long panniers. The crinoline is a descendant of these garments.

Crinolines are often associated with the gothic look; as with corsets, they can transport one instantly back in time. The crinoline is a cage-like garment worn under the skirt to give it volume. Due to the increased ease of mass production, they were widely worn across society, whereas in previous generations farthingales and panniers had only been available to the wealthy,

1840s fashion plate, French, Rijksmuseum.

Mary Carrick Riggs is wearing a black and purple dress, with a crinoline to widen her skirts, 1857, Metropolitan Museum of Art.

Woman in black Taffeta Dress and Lace Shawl, c.1850, Metropolitan Museum of Art.

As painted by John Everett Millais in 1854, art critic John Ruskin wearing frock coat and trousers.

and those lower down the social ladder had had to make do with padded bum rolls and petticoats stiffened with horsehair. Their wire shape is evocative of skeletons, and their width was supposedly a fire hazard as the skirt could easily catch alight without being instantly noticed. A massive skirt helped emphasis the coveted small waist beloved by Victorian fashionistas. Crinolines still feature in modern-day bridal wear, and they enjoyed a revival as the 'Mini-Crini' in Vivienne Westwood's famous 1985 collection, which influenced the puff ball skirt fashions of the 1980s.

Perhaps we see the Victorian era through a gothic lens, as black-and-white photographs make it appear gloomier than it actually was. On the contrary, William Henry Perkin invented the first synthetic aniline dye in 1856, allowing colours to become more exaggerated and extreme. The first of these was 'mauveine', a huge signature colour of the decade as people went wild for this rich, never-before-seen shade of purple.

By the end of the decade, other dyes such as crimson were being pioneered, making fabrics darker and richer and more vibrant than they had ever been before. Purple is a very gothic colour; perhaps it remains a favourite with goths today because of its associations with both the Victorians and mourning wear. A stereotypical goth wears all black, but many choose to mix other colours with their black outfits. Some choose white; others, red or purple – all classic goth colours thanks to their associations with death, nobility and the Victorians. In more recent years, goths

and cybergoths have chosen neon colours, impossible to produce without the development of chemical dyes.

Sleeves on womenswear became wider and more sweeping, a nod to the medieval. Shoulders dropped, making bodices look softer, but waists remained small, albeit with less tight lacing. White collars and cuffs were in fashion. Fringing, tassels, flounces and other trims were in vogue for decorating skirts and bodices during this decade – all of which feature in Lolita fashion (a modern Japanese subculture interested in Victorian styles).

Separate bodices and skirts were often used; even if an outfit looked like a single item, it was often made of several pieces. Bodices of this type are still fashionable in gothic circles and also influence modern gothic jackets.

Lace-up ankle boots were popular for women. Before the 1810s, shoes were not specifically made for the right or left foot – the wearer simply broke them in. After this period, however, boots became much sturdier, another gothic staple.

The development of the crinoline also saw the appearance of long ankle-length drawers (also called bloomers) to prevent too much flesh being revealed if crinolines lifted up. Until the Regency period, knickers, bloomers or any other type of underwear were not widely worn; women would be bare save for their underskirts. Some bloomers would be crotchless to make going to the toilet easier. The American women's rights advocate Amelia Bloomer tried to pioneer women's trousers at this time; they didn't catch on, but the seeds were sown, and the style of her bloomer trousers was echoed in the cycling outfits which appeared later in the nineteenth century, as well as the Lolita and steampunk styles.

The invention and mass production by Singer of the sewing machine by the 1850s allowed people to make more complex clothes at home, and sewing patterns for home use grew in popularity.

Menswear

Sewing machines made ready-to-wear men's clothes more easily available. Dark hues were still fashionable for men, although lighter colours were acceptable in summer. White shirts and jaunty neckties became fashionable, and bowler hats were introduced.

Frock coats with skirts were also fashionable, as were top hats; the sack back (loose-fitting) jacket, which had appeared in the 1840s, continued to grow in popularity. Tailcoats were popular in formal daywear and are still much romanticised by goths, inspiring many modern goth jackets and coats.

The 1850s saw Levi Strauss first make his denim trousers for Gold Rush workers, trousers which would eventually become known as jeans. Now worn universally, they started as workwear, and by the middle of the twentieth century were seen as a sign of youthful rebellion. A twenty-first-century goth's wardrobe now commonly includes black jeans and denim.

1860s

As previously mentioned, the 1860s saw the death of Prince Albert, and mourning culture became more extreme.

Womenswear

Crinolines reached the peak of their size in the early 1860s, some reaching twelve feet in circumference. Their shape began to change in 1862; they became flattened at the front but spread out at the back. Thanks to faster and more efficient production methods, they became affordable for all classes (although some servants were still obliged to wear the out-of-date round ones).

By the late 1860s, 'half hoops', a forerunner to the bustle, which only gave volume at the back, spread in popularity. Again, like crinolines, bustles can be seen

Funerale, Pierre-Louis Pierson, 1860s,
Metropolitan Museum of Art.

Walking dress, c.1865, American,
Metropolitan Museum of Art.

Skirts were multi-layered by the mid-1860s and drawn up to show decorative underskirts in different colours with ruffles.

in gothic fashion today and also feature heavily in steampunk fashion. Even if they don't feature as whole pieces of underwear, they often inspire additional frills and flounces on goth skirts and dresses. Skirts were multilayered by the mid-1860s and drawn up to show decorative underskirts in different colours with ruffles. Corsets became shorter as the waist climbed upwards.

Women began to wear blouses inspired by men's military shirts, especially the Garibaldi shirt inspired by the Italian freedom fighter; its rebellious, romantic connotations were very gothic indeed! Modern gothic jackets and shirts are often inspired by military wear, especially military uniforms from the eighteenth and nineteenth centuries.

Jackets were worn with three-quarter-length coats with wide skirts and paisley shawls. Jackets from this period tend to look very gothic, as do mantles (sculptured shawls decorated with tassels and trimmings).

Bonnets shrank, and hats were placed on the centre rather than the side of the head. They often featured netting resembling a miniature veil, reminiscent of the gothic veil, a sign of mourning and mystery. To the modern eye, these resemble the fascinators and hats favoured by the femme fatales of the 1940s.

Menswear

Menswear was loose, with baggy trousers and three-quarter-length jackets providing a somewhat relaxed look. Sack or lounge jackets became very popular (resembling blazers and smoking jackets); tailcoats were now only for evening wear, and it became an absolute no-no to match your waistcoat to your jacket.

Various men's coats and jackets, which have gone on to influence gothic fashion for both men and women, became fashionable in this era. They include the Chesterfield coat, with braiding and velvet facings; the short double-breasted reefer; and the Inverness, with its attached cape. The cape was still acceptable for men's evening outerwear – perhaps it is so strongly associated with the gothic because it was still being worn in this golden age of gothic literature. As genre fiction novels were still a relatively new phenomenon (the gothic novel was just over a hundred years old

Mens fashion plate, 1864, Rijksmuseum.

A military man relaxing, sporting a moustache and a stylish
uniform, painted by James Jacques Joseph Tissot in 1870.

at this point), the genre (and its subgenres of horror) was still developing; no wonder we still use fashions and conventions from this time, when the norms of gothic and supernatural characters were still being developed.

Military wear had an influence on men's fashion, with the mass production of army uniforms in the American Civil War. British soldiers' military tailoring and facial hair was widely imitated by the male population.

The top hat, like the crinoline, reached its peak in the early 1860s before decreasing in popularity over the decade, gradually being replaced by the bowler hat.

Alice in Wonderland

Alice's Adventures in Wonderland was published in 1865. The book has provided much inspiration for gothic fashion in the late twentieth and early twenty-first centuries, with its puffed skirts, layers of petticoats and top hats. Film adaptations such as Tim Burton's *Alice in Wonderland* and Zack Snyder's *Sucker Punch* (a retelling set in an insane asylum) have become increasingly gothic. *Alice*'s influence can be seen on gothic Lolita, Victorian-style goths and steampunks. At its heart, *Alice* could even be seen as a gothic text, a girl lost in a strange land populated by sinister and mysterious figures.

1870s

Womenswear

The 1870s saw bustles take hold: structured undergarments which emphasised the back of a woman's skirt, made either from wire or thick horsehair. Other items did a very similar job, such as the crinolette. Just like the crinoline, these undergarments have a skeletal look to them and feature as outerwear in modern gothic fashion. Womenswear became highly decorative during this period, bustles being

The Shower of Cards by John Tenniel, from *Alice in Wonderland*, British Library.

Wedding ensemble, 1878, Metropolitan Museum of Art.

very exaggerated, with frills and flounces with lots of draping and layering (a style known as polonaise).

Necklines became more open, allowing more space for necklaces (made of jet in mourning wear) and chokers. The choker is the ultimate in gothic neck attire, not only because of its name's ghoulish connotations but also its association with vampires (a choker can be used to cover up a vampire bite!) and guillotine victims. In modern imagination, chokers are often associated with Victorian fashion.

The late 1870s saw the development of fitted figure-hugging gowns (with bustles and trains at the back), a fashion staple ever since. There had been earlier trends for fitted bodices, but narrow skirts were a novel idea. This look can be seen as a template for femmes fatales and gothic vamps in the early years of Hollywood: a tradition still with us today when we think of gothic beauties such as Morticia Addams.

Lillie Langtry, the 'Jersey Lily', a British-American socialite, accidently created a sensation. She has been credited with popularising the little black dress; she wore a very simple, unadorned black dress to a society dinner party, as she was in mourning

Afternoon dress, House of Worth, 1872, Metropolitan Museum of Art. Dress by Charles Frederick Worth, often described as the pioneer of haute couture. He was a British designer who made his name in Paris. Many of his designs feature swirling black patterns in blacks, purples and whites, and can therefore look very gothic.

A Jersey Lily (portrait of Lillie Langtry),
Sir John Everett Millais, 1878.

for her brother. However, instead of shrinking into the background, her simple beauty made her a sensation. She was painted by John Everett Millais and caught the attention of the Prince of Wales, eventually becoming his mistress. She went on to have a successful acting career. It just goes to show the power of the black dress!

Portrait of a lady, c.1876–1880, Yale University Library.

Men's Fashion

In the 1870s, men's fashion was subtle and loose-fitting, in contrast to the exaggerated women's fashion. Smoking jackets and knee-length Chesterfields were popular, as were bowler hats, sack suits, cravats and pocket watches. The influence on today's gothic and steampunk dandies is very evident.

Portrait of a lady, late 1870s.

Afternoon dress, 1880s,
Metropolitan Museum of Art.

Portia (1886) by Sir John Everett Millais, Metropolitan
Museum of Art. There is something vampiric about her
high-necked red gown and cloak-like robe.

Fashion plate, 1885, Rijksmuseum.

Corset, 1880s,
Galleries of the
Metropolitan
Museum of Art.

Tulipes Hollandaises cape, House of Worth, 1889,
Metropolitan Museum of Art. A high-necked black cloak
decorated with tulips, designed by Charles Frederick
Worth. Many Victorian fashions like this have become
associated with gothic characters such as vampires,
because they featured in the fiction of the time.

1880s

Womenswear

Dresses remained tight and fitted. Bustles continued
to be highly decorative and influenced by the 1700s,
with their multiple layers and decorations. Waistcoats
and high collars became fashionable in what was
known as the 'Dolly Varden' look, after the actress
who wore this style.

Fashion plate, 1894, Rijksmuseum.

Menswear

Deerstalkers, as popularised by Sherlock Holmes, were worn in the countryside. The three-piece lounge suit (very similar to its modern equivalent) was fashionable. Suits came in tartan, plaid and check fabrics. Collars were buttoned high. The covert coat – a short overcoat, often with velvet lapels, became popular in the middle of the decade.

The Aesthetic Movement also developed during this decade. It was consciously influenced by history, prized artistic beauty and stood apart from mainstream fashion; it was, in fact, anti-fashion, and counted Oscar Wilde and William Morris amongst its devotees. It was, arguably, a type of early subculture; its unusual ideas about fashion and lifestyle have influenced later twentieth-century subcultures such as goths and hippies.

1890s

Womenswear

The 1890s heralded a change in shapes: long bell-shaped skirts took on a more natural shape. Lacy, frothy blouses and puffed gigot sleeves were all the rage. The influence of these blouses on goth fashion is clear to see. The number of women in the workplace doubled, so more combinations of blouses and jackets (fitted jackets with puffed sleeves to accommodate the blouses) arose, providing inspiration for the modern steampunk look. Some women even began to wear cycling two-pieces, complete with trousers/bloomers, another steampunk inspiration.

Fashion plate, 1894, Rijksmuseum.

Menswear

Narrow frock coats were fashionable for daywear and tailcoats for evening wear, while the tuxedo had grown in popularity. Both bowler hats and top hats were still worn. Long overcoats were also in fashion. Knickerbockers, similar to breeches, were popular for country pursuits, as interest grew in sport as a leisure activity.

Evening jacket, House of Worth, c.1890,
Metropolitan Museum of Art. A stunning
men's jacket designed by Charles Frederick
Worth. This dramatic, decadent style was
championed by the Aesthetic Movement, who
were often mocked for their theatrical style.

Sir John Everett Millais, wearing a medieval-style hood, dressed as Dante.

MEDIEVAL AND GOTHIC REVIVAL IN ART AND STYLE

The Pre-Raphaelite movement began in the middle of the nineteenth century with a small group of artists including Dante Gabriel Rossetti, William Holman Hunt, Edward Burne-Jones and John Everett Millais. It lasted for five years, but its influence continued for the rest of the century, with the artists' work becoming increasingly in demand. They rejected the mainstream art and culture of their day, finding it too insipid and sentimental, and instead took their inspiration from Italian painters working before Raphael, hence their name.

They painted dramatic, striking and moody pictures and were inspired by the Bible, Shakespeare and medieval lore, often involving troubling subtexts. Their muses were mostly handsome, strong-looking women rather than the pretty, shrinking angels of the home so beloved of Victorian society. Goddesses, witches and magical women from myths and legends often featured in their work but were portrayed as striking and attractive rather than wizened crones. These paintings celebrated forgotten times when magic was supposedly still possible.

William Morris was the most famous member of the Arts and Crafts movement, closely connected to the Pre-Raphaelites and the Aesthetic Movement. Morris focused on Gothic revival architecture and design, criticising the Industrial Revolution for its ruinous effect on the countryside and traditional crafts. Ironically, despite starting off as outsiders, the Arts and Crafts movement and their Gothic revivalist style

went on to inform much of our ideas about Victorian architecture. William Morris was a very successful artist, writer and designer by the time of his death.

These movements looked back to medieval styles and revived loose-fitting gowns and robes with sweeping sleeves but in darker, natural, earthier tones. Their paintings show people clothed in a romanticised medieval style, with dark, heavy colours and rich-looking fabrics; the wearers are often handsome, strong and, somehow, otherworldly in appearance. The detail on clothing is often meticulous. They wanted to celebrate natural beauty instead of trying to unnaturally mould women's shapes. They also appreciated the negative impact that tight and heavy clothes were having on women's health.

Liberty's of London opened in 1875, a department store that became linked to these movements. They imported decorative fabrics from Asia and began to sell Japanese fashions, including kimonos. The

Aesthetic Movement leapt on these styles as they felt they fitted with their ethos.

Elizabeth Siddal, the model and artist who married Dante Gabriel Rossetti, pioneered the fashion style that became associated with the Pre-Raphaelites by refusing to wear corsets or crinolines and opting for loose clothes in natural colours. Jane Burden, later to marry William Morris, also often wore looser dresses and was photographed wearing a Victorian dress without a crinoline, showing the beautiful folds of the free-flowing material.

The artist Aubrey Beardsley was also involved with the Aesthetic Movement. His spindly, dream-like engravings often show fantastical fashions which would be equally at home in sci-fi or fantasy. Either way, many of them are undeniably gothic.

Ironically, both mainstream Victorian fashion and the subculture of the Aesthetic Movement influence modern-day gothic fashion.

END OF AN ERA

Queen Victoria died in 1901, bringing to an end the Victorian age and ushering in the bright and decadent Edwardian age. Her long reign had seen huge advances in society and technology, tempered by a fear of change and massive disruption of the social order. This fed into the fiction and mood of the day, with Victorian society on one hand being rational, logical, scientific and reserved, while superstition, a fascination with the macabre and a fear of the consequences of discovering too much bubbled underneath – rather like *Jekyll and Hyde*.

Many of our storytelling archetypes derive from the Victorian era, when the most famous horror and gothic masterpieces were written. Photography and moving pictures were developed during the era, capturing these images and ideals, while the growth of literacy and printing presses allowed ideas and creative interactions, previously confined to the elite, to become part of the public imagination as popular culture grew as an idea. Therefore, the Victorians have left a permanent impression on us through the gothic stories, characters and ideas they passed down to us; the modern eye cannot help but see the gothic through a Victorian lens.

The Black Cape, for Salomé by Oscar Wilde, Aubrey Beardsley, 1906–7, Metropolitan Museum of Art.

Ophelia, John Everett Millais, 1851–2. For Millais's painting of Ophelia, Elizabeth Siddal modelled wearing a second-hand silver dress (which cost four pounds) in the bath. She caught a bad cold – a serious matter in the nineteenth century – after posing for too long in the cold water.

1900-1970

From Vamps to Punks: the Lead-Up to Goth

The dawn of the twentieth century was a time of excitement and trepidation. Technology evolved at an increasing rate, travel became easier and huge strides were made in women's rights and education. Queen Victoria saw in the first year of the new century, but died in 1901, bringing the Victorian age to an end. The coronation of her son, Edward, saw the official start of the Edwardian age (although some consider the Edwardian age to have begun stylistically in the 1890s, making it more contemporary with the French Belle Époque).

Dramatic events in the early decades of the twentieth century saw political systems challenged and reinvented with the rise of both Nazism and Communism, two world wars, the Spanish Flu sweeping through already fragile populations and,

Camille Gifford, *c.*1905, wearing the Gibson Girl style fashion.

in many countries, the efforts of women's suffrage groups rewarded with the vote. Cinema flourished, with films developing from silent, brief shots to long sweeping epics with dialogue, music, complicated plots and stunning costumes. Film became a multi-million-dollar industry and a greater influence on the way people dressed, from factory workers to aristocrats, than anything ever before. The avant garde movement of the 1920s involved greater artistic experimentation, which was embraced by the increasingly liberated youth. Growing numbers of people could read and write, fuelling the need for more reading material and increasing the popularity of pulp fiction and comic books.

The increase of fast fashion, with mass production in factories, made clothing cheaper. Fashion was no longer just the preserve of the wealthy, but people from all classes could indulge and develop their own personal styles.

With people spending longer in education, the idea of the protected childhood spread, and growing up was delayed. The teenager that we know today began to appear, and, by the 1960s, had become a beast in their own right, with opinions, attitude problems and a desire to form tribes and rebel.

NEW WOMEN, GIBSON GIRLS AND THE FIRST WORLD WAR

At the dawn of the new century, fashion was bright and frothy. Women wore long floor-length skirts that skimmed the waist and fell naturally without crinolines or bustles. Spectacular hats, trimmed and towering, took the place of skirts as the obviously impractical, extravagant garment. There were two iconic looks for women: the New Woman and The Gibson Girl.

The New Woman was likely to be a suffragette or at least have suffragette leanings. She may have been one of the small but growing number of young women attending university or working in traditionally male spheres, such as in an office, as a doctor or a journalist. Consequently, they dressed in a formal fashion, matching their skirts with men's smart jackets, waistcoats and ties. This androgyny is still celebrated in gothic fashion, with waistcoats and traditionally masculine-style coats frequently worn by both genders. In the same way, modern male goths sometimes wear skirts and make-up.

New Women backed the practical rational dress movement, which was in favour of more practical and hygienic clothes for men and women. The tweed they often sported was also later favoured by the punk designer Vivienne Westwood – and so-called corporate goths, as the look mixes professionalism with old world glamour and heritage. New Women tended to wear darker and more muted colours, hoping to be taken more seriously by men in their work or educational environment. It is easy to see how some of this has influenced gothic fashion; long black skirts are a simple and easy fashion to emulate, as are smart black jackets and blouses.

While many New Women were associated with tweeds and dark colours, the suffragettes had their own colour coding: white, green and purple in Britain. Purple was chosen for its noble connotations, emphasising what they saw as their noble crusade. Purple continued to be linked with royalty in the twentieth century but has also been appropriated by some alternative communities. The goth community uses it for its links with mourning and nobility.

The Gibson Girls were highly feminine, idealised versions of beautiful girls, and were often drawn by the artist Charles Gibson. They wore large, highly decorated hats featuring lace, ornaments, feathers and veils. They also wore the uncomfortable S-bend corset; most corsets are not necessarily uncomfortable and not designed to be tightly laced. Before the invention of elastic, they were merely supportive garments, but the S-bend was designed to shape the body solely with fashion in mind and little thought for comfort. It created a mono-bosom, forcing out the bosom and the bottom and giving the torso an S-bend shape. These distinctive corsets have influenced gothic and fetish fashions. The headwear, long skirts and frilly, frothy blouses of the Gibson Girls have heavily influenced goth fashion; while it would be rare to see a goth with an exact Gibson Girl hat, they nevertheless enjoy decorating their headgear with feathers and lace – albeit in much darker shades than the pretty pastels favoured by the Gibson Girls!

King Edward VII was a trendsetter for men's fashion and pioneered the tuxedo suit, originally in dark blue, before it became more widely popularised as the black version we know today. Suits were still the order of the day for Edwardian men, with skinny fitted trousers and jackets. Tailcoats were still worn for formal occasions and the bowler hat was often worn by professional working men. As previously mentioned, tailored men's suits are often copied by modern-day goths; the late Victorian/Edwardian dandy look is especially popular. As sport grew in popularity as a hobby, knitted jumpers and knickerbockers became popular.

As the first decade wore on, women's fashion saw the most significant changes. The hobble skirt appeared, a forerunner to the pencil skirt and a probable influence on tightly fitted vamp-style wear. They were tight at the ankle, causing women to hobble, hence their name. Skirts became shorter (although still near to the ankle) and designers such as Paul Poiret experimented with exotic looks including harem pants, again still embraced by alternative communities today.

Edward VII died in 1910, accompanied by much public mourning, especially at court. Victorian-style mourning would never be seen again after this, as the rest of the decade was overshadowed by the First World War. The mortality rate was so high that oppressive mourning culture and rituals just became too much. Keeping public morale high was everything and wearing mourning dress for lengthy periods was not a good look; people still wore black, but for a much shorter time. Many young people's illusions about the romance of war and the ideal of dying for one's country had been shattered by the mud and blood of trench warfare. We still wear blood-red poppies today to remember those who fell.

Vamp / Femme fatale.

The war affected fashion in other ways. Women dressed more practically, as they went out to work and took the jobs the fighting men left behind. Most men were conscripted and proudly wore the green uniforms of their regiments, complete with trench coat. Great coats and trench coats had been a staple of men's fashion since the early 1800s, but as the century progressed, their function changed from formal or military wear to alternative wear, and they were also more widely worn by women.

After the war, the Spanish flu struck, killing at least fifty million people worldwide, many of them young. Writing in 2021, with the Covid-19 pandemic still rumbling on, the effects of such a catastrophe are not hard to imagine. News of death from an invisible killer is everywhere; it helps us to understand how the constant proximity of death for earlier generations would have influenced folklore and gothic stories, feeding off ideas of sudden changes, transformations and people being struck down by contagions. (The legends of vampires, zombies and werewolves perhaps all stem from ideas about contagious diseases.)

1920s

The 1920s was a time of frivolity and rewriting the rules of society, a reaction to the tragedies of the 1910s. Feeling let down by the powers that be, a traumatised generation looked for new ways of living.

The corset had been abandoned and clothing became more liberated, with hemlines much higher than before, reaching only to the knee. Women's hairstyles also became shorter. More women wore trousers, although this had not yet become mainstream. These radical changes made it easier to experiment with fashion without fear of being socially ostracised.

The 1960s is celebrated as a rebellious decade, but the 1920s laid the groundwork. It was a time when young people broke away from the rules of a society that had failed them, a vital step towards the emergence of subcultures.

The so-called Bright Young Things were a group of socialites and bohemians around London who came to typify life in this sparkling decade. They lived life to the full, wore shocking clothes and partied, rebelling after the First World War.

Artists, musicians and writers from around the world flocked to Paris to pursue their artistic dreams and live non-traditional lifestyles. This has become known as the avant garde and included styles such as surrealism and Cubism.

Many female artists emerged in the 1920s and 1930s. Some experimented with fashion, taking inspiration from across the world and throughout history. Winifred Knights was inspired by Italian peasants. Frida Kahlo celebrated the national dress of her native Mexico and fused it with items from China, India and beyond. Her striking style featured on the cover of *Vogue*, and when she walked down the street on a visit to the United States, children followed her, entranced. She was known to occasionally dress as a man, and celebrated her thick eyebrows and faint moustache: the complete opposite to Western beauty standards of the time. Leonor Fini, another cross-dressing artist, dyed her hair a variety of colours, including blue, and was known to wear only a feather cape and a pair of boots when attending parties. Georgia O'Keeffe, whose more famous subject matters included bones and flowers, understood the power of dressing in monochrome to make a more striking impression in publicity shots.

Salvador Dali, one of the most famous surrealists, with his crafted moustache and works featuring clocks and skulls, has plenty of gothic-inclined fans. His forays into fashion included working with the experimental fashion designer Elsa Schiaparelli.

Schiaparelli was a rival to Coco Chanel, at the opposite end of the style spectrum; while Chanel dressed down, Schiaparelli dressed up. Chanel's style would have seemed experimental to her contemporaries, but Schiaparelli's garments are now more shocking to the modern eye. She experimented with shapes, patterns, colours and prints like few others. One of her most obviously gothic creations was the 1938 skeleton evening dress, a collaboration with Salvador Dali. It was a long, fitted black evening gown, with padding across the ribs, hips and down the legs, giving the impression of bones. While Chanel made black cool, Schiaparelli incorporated the surreal and the theatrical into her designs. Goths owe both a debt of gratitude.

By the 1920s, black was still worn for mourning but had taken on a new meaning thanks to the young French designer Coco Chanel. Preferring a much less complicated style than previous decades, she pioneered simple dresses for women. People went wild for her looser, shorter dresses – a clear departure from the past. She also favoured plainer, simpler colours – most famously black, which she made chic, fashionable, desirable and sexy – completely changing its Victorian and earlier connotations of mourning and professional wear. People actually wanted to wear black, and her 'little black dress', or LBD, is still with us today as a style staple.

Trousers and Jeans

Women started to wear trousers more often in the 1920s, and they became acceptable beachwear in the form of baggy beach pyjamas. The fashion elite wore wide palazzo pants, but trousers didn't become mainstream for women until the mid-twentieth century.

Men also embraced baggy trousers, known as Oxford bags; sporty knickerbockers were prohibited at Oxford University in the 1920s, so students began to wear ridiculously oversized trousers to conceal them, and the fashion caught on. Trousers fitted to extremes – whether too baggy or too tight – were, arguably, a sign of twentieth-century teenage rebellion.

Jeans switched from workwear to fashionable casual wear in the 1950s. In the 1960s, teenagers continued to rebel by wearing casual clothes. The

Woman dressed in a vintage Hollywood-inspired look. She has the appearance of a vamp or femme fatale. This villainous female character is a clever seductress; her darkly glamorous style has inspired sophisticated gothic fashion.

shape of jeans changed over the decades from the exaggerated bell bottoms of the 1970s to the skinny drainpipes of the 1980s and the baggy 'skater' jeans of the 2000s. Goths wear many of these styles, but are most synonymous with the black skinny jean (as are their twenty-first-century offspring: the emo).

Colour-Coding Children

The idea of pink for baby girls and blue for baby boys is a twentieth-century concept. In earlier centuries, clothes had been passed down through families regardless of colour – families tended to have large numbers of children and infant mortality rates were high. By the twentieth century, families were becoming smaller and infant mortality rates were dropping. Department stores, keen as ever to make money from children's clothes, began to market blue for boys and pink for girls. By the 1920s and 1930s, this idea was becoming widely accepted as not only normal but traditional. Pink and blue are not colours overly associated with goths; the black or other dark colours they prefer reject any societal norms about gender.

More recently, gothic Lolita and perky goths (goths who tend to have more cute personae, incorporating bright colours and cartoonish prints alongside their black clothes) increasingly use pink as a secondary colour, especially in the hair. Peacock shades have been embraced by the goth community, especially those who mimic Victorian or Renaissance styles, with darker shades of blue joining purple in goth fashion.

The Silver Screen

The impact of cinema on gothic fashion cannot be underestimated. Before cinema, people who read or listened to gothic stories would have imagined the clothes, the monsters and the heroes slightly differently, regardless of how thorough the descriptions were. Paintings and illustrations also suggested how gothic characters should look, but few had access to them. The twentieth century changed all of this.

Many people wanted to copy stylish and glamorous film stars and the outfits they wore, including those featuring in 'shudder' or gothic films (the term 'horror film' wasn't coined until later). In the early days of the film industry, in the 1910s and 1920s, many books were made into films, which, along with art, illustrations, comic books and, of course, fashion, revealed how certain stock characters, heroes, villains and supernatural creatures should look, especially characters from well-known stories or books who have graced the silver screen time and time again.

As ever, the public had an appetite for the macabre, and frightening and so-called 'shudder' films became popular. The actors and actresses who starred in them became famous; despite often being typecast, they made huge names for themselves and became style-setters for gothic fashion today. Famous aristocrats of the time inspired gothic movie-star looks (in the same way that famous aristocrats had set styles in previous centuries); the Italian eccentric Luisa Amman wore white make-up with dark circles around her eyes at a time when a natural look was more fashionable. This, coupled with her experimental, dark fashion sense and exploits such as keeping big cats as pets, made her notorious.

Some of the original gothic movie stars either became trendsetters intentionally by matching their off-screen personae with the characters they played on film, or simply by being the first actor to take on a major role and make it their own. Some of the most noteworthy of such actors are discussed below.

Theda Bara

The word 'vamp' was, in fact, first applied to Theda Bara (née Theodosia Goodman), who found fame in the mid-1910s. Inspired by ancient Egypt, she would encircle her large eyes with heavy make-up and pair it with blood-red lipstick.

While her look was certainly not mainstream, Theda's allure was undeniable. Often playing a villain or a seductress, her roles included a vampire and Cleopatra. She associated herself with the mystical and dark world of Egyptian mythology, even claiming to have been born next to a sphinx!

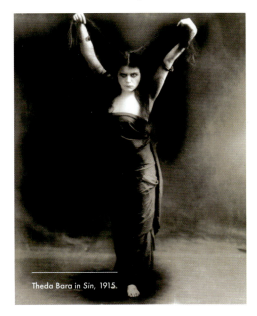

Theda Bara in *Sin*, 1915.

Film poster for *The She-Devil*, 1918. Film poster featuring Theda Bara, who was known as a vamp, a female character-type that featured in gothic films. They were often fallen or sexy women who were associated with darkness, wearing revealing, figure-hugging clothes.

It set the template for countless other horror films which followed.

Max Schreck and Greta Schröder

The 1922 German film *Nosferatu* is iconic among movie fans. It is a German retelling of Bram Stoker's *Dracula*. Max Schreck plays Graf Orlok, an eerily other-worldly-looking vampire, with long fingers, dark, heavily made-up eyes and a dark, long coat with a high collar. Greta Schröder plays the heroine, complete with long ringlets, dark eyes and nineteenth-century dress. It set the template for countless other horror films which followed, as well as reinforcing the link between nineteenth-century dress and the gothic.

Lon Chaney

Lon Chaney applied all his own make-up, which was often fantastical and extreme. He is well known for playing characters such as the Phantom of the Opera and the Hunchback of Notre Dame.

Film poster for *London After Midnight*
starring Lon Chaney, 1927.

Bela Lugosi in *Dracula*, 1931.

Bela Lugosi

No 'who's who' of gothic film actors would be complete without mentioning Bela Lugosi in the *Dracula* film of 1931. His portrayal of a dinner-suited Dracula remains the iconic image of Bram Stoker's anti-hero to this day. He played the role twice, as well as Ygor in *Son of Frankenstein* and two other cinematic vampires. He was tall, dark and handsome, as many goths aspire to be today, and lends his name to the famous gothic anthem *Bela Lugosi's Dead* by Bauhaus. Goths still visit his grave today. He was said to have been buried in his Dracula cloak.

Boris Karloff and Elsa Lanchester

Boris Karloff starred as the monster in *Frankenstein* (1931), catapulting him into gothic stardom. He would reprise the role twice more, featuring in two additional Frankenstein films. He played Imhotep in *The Mummy* (1932) as well as an array of other villains up to the 1960s.

Elsa Lanchester starred opposite Karloff in *The Bride of Frankenstein* (1935). Not only did she play the title role, but she also played Mary Shelley. Her tall beehive hairstyle was reminiscent of ancient Egypt and made her something of a horror icon. Her image

Bride of Frankenstein, 1935.

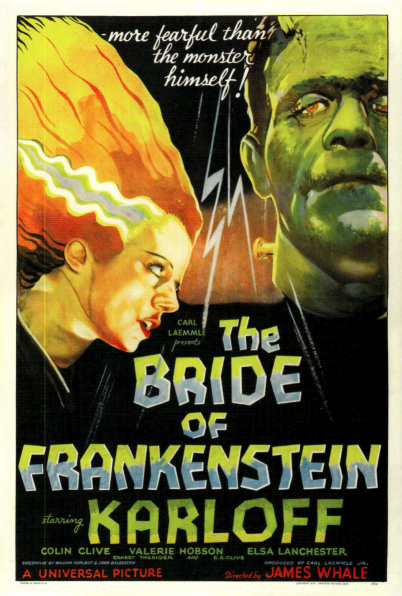

often appears on movie memorabilia, and her hair has been copied by costume designers and goths alike. In recent years, goth style-queen Daphne Guinness has been seen sporting her black-and-white hair in a beehive style.

Carrol Borland

Carrol Borland was a Dracula fan whose dreams came true when she starred with Bela Lugosi in another bloodsucking feature film, *Mark of the Vampire* (1935). She played Luna, the vampire's daughter. Her white gown was reminiscent of Philip Burne-Jones's painting *The Vampire* (1897), and her long black hair is a gothic trademark.

Cinema cemented the gothic characters of Victorian fiction as horror, archetypes, and their costumes reached a much wider audience. Attempts to replicate nineteenth-century costumes were sometimes more theatrical than accurate, but these fantastical takes on historical costumes helped to form the goth look later in the twentieth century.

While in Bram Stoker's novel Dracula was described as wearing all black, it was a 1920s theatrical interpretation which dressed him in a suit and inspired the costume designer for the silver screen.

The blacks, reds, greens and purples featured on dramatic horror film posters are still associated with gothic fashion today. Red often symbolises blood or danger in Western culture; purple is associated with alternative cultures; green and purple together resemble the colours of bruises; green can suggest rottenness or something otherworldly. Black and white films lend themselves well to the gothic genre, of course, as they emphasise shadows, dark colours and the scary nature of the surroundings.

Carrol Borland as Luna in *Mark of the Vampire*, 1935.

Carolyn Jones, the original Morticia Addams, became a touchstone for the gothic style.

Yvonne De Carlo as Lily Munster.

TELEVISION AND COMIC BOOKS

As television sets became cheaper and more accessible from the 1930s to the 1960s, they had the same effect as cinema in creating stock character types.

Gothic and horror characters began to appear on TV sets in people's front rooms, often in family-friendly formats. The most famous of these horror sitcoms, *The Addams Family*, started life in 1938 as a comic strip. The character of Morticia Addams was inspired by vamps and went on to inspire many more. *The Addams Family* made it onto TV screens in 1964, with matriarch Morticia being played as a glamorous witch by Carolyn Jones.

Her long figure-hugging dress, with draped sleeves and a low neck, is still the height of gothic fashion. She is an inspiration for goths and Halloween costumes alike, as well as being a byword for female goths. There have been many stage shows and film adaptations since the TV series, Anjelica Huston's portrayal of Morticia in the 1991 and 1993 films in *The Addams Family* (1991) and *Addams Family Values* (1993) being two of the most famous; pretty good for a TV series which was canned after its second season!

The Addams's daughter, Wednesday, has also inspired younger-style goth fashion and gothic Lolita with her black dresses, Peter Pan collars and long dark braids. The 2022 Netflix series *Wednesday* has seen a huge resurgence in all things Wednesday Addams with Jenna Ortega taking the title role. Lurch the butler and Morticia's husband Gomez wear the traditional dark suits associated with gothic men.

The Munsters was a direct rival to *The Addams Family* in the 1960s. Matriarch Lily Munster looks more like the Bride of Frankenstein from the 1935 film, with her black-and-white streaked hair and flowing gown. Yvonne de Carlo's iconic green make-up took three hours to apply. Both Lily and Morticia were beautiful, but gothic nevertheless, with their long dark hair, red lips, arched eyebrows and gowns which were more costume than fashion, yet still complementary to their figures.

The character of Vampira is more famous in the USA. A television presenter and B-movie actress, she was the alter-ego of Maila Nurmi, who went to an LA fancy-dress party as Morticia Addams in 1953. She caught the attention of film and media types at the party and was offered work, as long as she stayed in character. She evolved her costume into Vampira, taking inspiration from cartoon witches and fetish models.

The link between the fetish and burlesque scene and the gothic is still strong today. Both enjoy the darker side of vintage fashion. The 1950s saw a large fetish scene, a tantalisingly dark underbelly contrasting with the wholesome feel of the rest of the decade. Echoes of this live on, informing alternative culture from goths to rockabillies, psychobillies and vintage guys and girls.

Hammer Film Productions churned out horror films from the late 1950s to the early 1980s and also remade horror classics. Dracula was played by Christopher Lee played Dracula, a role which made him famous. *The Curse of Frankenstein*, Hammer's adaptation of Shelley's *Frankenstein*, was set in the nineteenth century; the beautiful heroine wore floaty, inaccurate period costumes, once again serving as an inspiration for gothic fashion. By the 1970s, Hammer was also making TV specials; while they were seen as

Vampira: Morticia Addams's influence is clear, but note the fetish flourishes, with the long nails and tiny waist.

Poster for the 1960 Hammer film *Brides of Dracula*, complete with gothic colour palette, floaty dresses and a cape.

both scary and sexy at the time, they have lost much of their terror for modern audiences, and their treatment of scantily clad women has not aged well.

Peter Cushing, Christopher Lee and Vincent Price also featured in 1960s horror films and television programmes, firmly establishing the tall, dark aristocrat as a gothic villain.

Comic strips and, more recently, graphic novels, are another visual medium which grew in popularity from the early twentieth century onwards. They resemble penny dreadfuls and pulp fiction with

their dramatic plots and larger-than-life characters, mixing elements of horror, crime, thrillers and sci-fi. Many have been adapted into TV shows and films, with the characters becoming folklore figures for the modern day. Portrayals of the villains are often gothic, including capes and heavy make-up, and, in the case of the women, dark clingy dresses.

Batman is one of the most famous comic book characters and definitely one of the most gothic. You don't need to stretch your imagination to see his links with vampires; he's rich, he often changes identity

Eartha Kitt as Catwoman in the 1960s TV show.

the orphaned acrobat, the Joker and Harley Quinn, with their darker takes on circus outfits and make-up. Thanks to twentieth-century horror films, the portrayals of freak shows and circuses have become increasingly gothic, and the performers' costumers – stripy tights, tutus, corsets and heavy make-up – resemble gothic, burlesque and fetish fashion.

FETISH FASHION

In the 1950s, John Sutcliffe invented the catsuit, made using latex rubber. Rubber, originally a practical early form of waterproofing from South America, was used in Britain during the nineteenth century and had already acquired an underground fetish following. The 1950s saw a growth in the appetite for fetish wear and images, perhaps as a reaction against the prim and proper values of the time.

The catsuit was designed as a fetish garment and was a big success. It crossed over into mainstream culture when Diana Rigg wore one as Emma Peel in the popular 1960s TV show *The Avengers*; from then on, it has been associated with both superheroines and villainesses – especially Catwoman, of course.

Some of the underground fetish stars of the 1950s became notorious due both to their popularity and censorship court cases. Bettie Page is the most well known and is now a byword for sexy Fifties style. Her look – black hair and fringe, teamed with a tight pencil skirt, a waist clincher, a bullet bra and high heels – inspired plenty of alternative girls through the years, including punks, the direct forerunners to

at night; and there are the obvious links to bats and his Batcave. His dark outfit, complete with boots and cape, is part of gothic fashion and the bat symbol features on many T-shirts worn by goths and non-goths alike. His enemy/love interest is the equally gothic Catwoman, a beautiful woman in a tightly fitted black outfit, dressed as the witch's familiar of choice. The circus is never far away either, with Robin

Theda Bara in *Cleopatra*, full costume, 1917.

goths. Rockabillies, another relation to goths, were also influenced heavily by this look. Dita von Teese, the twenty-first-century burlesque superstar, as well as goth and fetish pin-up, is the modern face of this movement and has acknowledged Bettie Page as an influence on her style. The fetish touches gives the vintage look a dark edge, so it is a style emulated by many glamorous modern-day goth women.

Women in gothic novels have often been sexualised, whether because of their virginity or their status as sexually active villainesses. The crossover between fetish fashion and the gothic is, therefore, hardly surprising.

ANCIENT EGYPT, THE OCCULT AND WICCANS

The 1920s saw a fashion for everything ancient Egyptian, sparked by contemporary archaeological discoveries in Egypt, especially Howard Carter's dig in 1922, when he discovered a treasure haul at the tomb of Tutankhamun.

Over the next ten years, Carter oversaw the removal of hundreds of items to Britain. The find made him world-famous, and he spent the years until his death in 1939 writing and giving talks about ancient Egypt and archaeology. Rumours about a curse on the tomb began as soon as it was discovered and weren't helped when several of those connected with the dig died in mysterious circumstances – including Lord Carnarvon, whose death in Cairo coincided with a power cut. This made Carter's discovers all the more exciting and provided the burgeoning film industry with an opportunity to make

The gothic heavily pencilled eye was originally inspired by the ancient Egyptians.

the mummy a creature of terror – a new addition to the gothic genre. Whilst the Greeks and Romans are famous for their temples and auditoriums, the Egyptians are famous for how they treated their dead and their pyramid burials, so they have long held a fascination for those of a gothic leaning.

The 'mummy' look has inspired fashion designers such as Alexander McQueen and the singer Amy Lee, who has worn a bandage-inspired dress.

The clothes that feature on ancient Egyptian hieroglyphics are striking and dramatic – especially their headwear and make-up. The gothic heavily pencilled eye was originally inspired by the ancient Egyptians. Film star vamps such as Theda Bara adopted the look and invented links to Egypt. Symbols such as the Eye of Horus made their way into 1920s design and jewellery and still are used in goth clothes today. Generally, goth jewellery tends to be silver – more of a reference to Celtic jewellery, but many goths will make an exception for ancient Egyptian-style gold jewellery. The ancient Egyptians also valued cats very highly, much like witches and their familiars. Cats are still a popular pet of choice for today's goths.

An interest in the occult was no longer taboo; in fact, it was a craze. The Victorian fascination with seances did not go away. The interest in ancient Egypt during the 1920s added further fuel to this, due to the association with Egyptian mummies and tombs. With the fallout from the First World War, it is hardly surprising that people wanted to contact loved ones who had gone beyond the veil.

Once such person inspired by the ancient Egyptians was the infamous Aleister Crowley. In the early 1920s, he established his own religion, called 'Thelema', in which he cherry-picked belief systems from other cultures and from what he had learnt as a member of other secret occult societies. He went by various names, including '666 The Beast', a biblical reference which has ended up as a slogan on many goth T-shirts and jewellery. Crowley's own version of

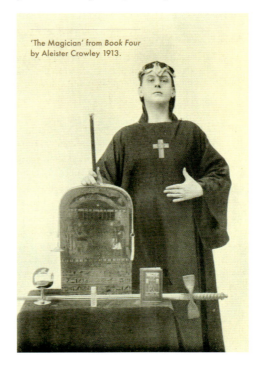

'The Magician' from *Book Four* by Aleister Crowley 1913.

Dark lipstick and dramatic
make-up favoured by goths.

the tarot deck has become popular. Tarot imagery is often used on goth clothing and jewellery; in fact, you could say a tarot deck is a perfect goth accessory.

It is worth noting the Wiccan religion, which was born in the 1940s. It draws heavily on pagan traditions, or what we envision pagan traditions to be, as well as folk practices.

While Wicca is a modern religion, its links to the ancient world and accompanying images of druids and priestesses wearing hooded robes with sweeping sleeves have influenced both hippie and goth fashion. Slogans and images associated with Wiccan practices are also widely produced on goth jewellery, T-shirts and accessories. The development of the T-shirt (which evolved from underwear in 1904 and was named by Scott Fitzgerald in the 1920s) is important to many modern goths' wardrobes. A dark T-shirt with an image associated with witchcraft or the occult communicates goth strongly and clearly!

MAKE-UP

Make-up grew into an enormous global industry in the twentieth century. It was previously unavailable to the poorer members of society, but lips and cheeks could be reddened using natural resources such as fruits and flowers.

The First World War created a need to put on a brave face and a smile for the troops. What better way to achieve this than through make-up? The growth of the film industry also showed the public what looks could be achieved with make-up, and the 1920s was

a time for very dramatic make-up, including dark lipstick, sometimes applied differently from the natural lip shape. Dark lipstick was often associated with vamps and villains and paler shades with more innocent girls. Dark eye make-up had similar associations. The make-up of the 1940s and 1950s featured cat-eye shapes and bold lips. Male glam rockers of the 1970s experimented with dramatic make-up.

Make-up, like fashion, was now available more widely and cheaply due to fast fashion and new and ever-evolving discoveries of chemicals and synthetic materials. It was much safer to wear than it had been in the past and therefore it was also less risky to experiment with to achieve a more dramatic look. Noticeable and experimental make-up is key to the modern goth look.

TEENAGERS, SUBCULTURES AND MUSIC

The 1950s saw the evolution of the modern teenager. Teenagers had more free time than previous generations because they spent longer in education. They used it to get involved in music and fashion. Rebellious rock-and-roll music became popular. They were the first generation after the Second World War to grown up mostly without rationing, and so could not understand why their parents were so frugal. They wanted to change Britain into a vibrant, cool country, as they thought it had become dull and shabby.

As we have seen in previous centuries, groups of rebels have always existed on the sidelines – often groups of young people forming new artistic circles.

However, it was only in the twentieth century that a subculture's ideas, dress and music were able to spread more widely. Subcultures became linked with teenagers trying to rebel and forming their own tribes, by identifying themselves with certain styles of dress and music which were contrary to the mainstream (although, retrospectively, they came to define a certain era or became absorbed into the mainstream).

One of the earliest modern British subcultures was the Teddy Boy, so called because they emulated Edwardian dress, including smart jackets, ties, shirts with high collars and fitted trousers. It would not have been difficult to obtain second-hand Edwardian clothes in the 1950s.

London has long been a leader in men's fashion, especially since Charles II pioneered a forerunner to the three-piece suit in the 1600s and Beau Brummell shook up the Georgian macaroni style with his toned-back Regency elegance. Savile Row, a destination for well-dressed men since the 1700s, had a hand in the creation of the Teddy Boys. In the early 1950s, Savile Row tailors began to reproduce Edwardian-style suits for their wealthy clientele. They became more popular with gangs of working-class lads, who saw them as status symbols and would pay for them in instalments. The long coats were also handy for hiding contraband goods such as knives and booze. It wasn't long before the Teddy Boys were mixing Edwardian styles with looks from the American rock-and-roll scene, itself influenced by styles from Western movies (with bolo and colonel ties).

Although they got themselves a bad name for being rowdy and violent, they were one of the first distinctive subcultures to really focus on dress as a way of standing out, as well as adapting fashions from the past. While goths and Teddy Boys are very different, goth fashion also frequently borrows inaccurately from and re-invents and romanticises the past.

Teddy Boys loved their hair, applying grease to make it pliable for their desired quiffs and twists. Extreme hairstyles have resonated with many subcultures since, especially punks and goths, known for their spiked and dyed locks.

The style spread through the UK until it became synonymous with the 1950s British teenager, and was featured heavily in the press (the *Daily Express* first coined the term 'Teddy Boys'). They saw resurgences in the 1970s, 1980s, and 2000s with rockabillies being heavily influenced by their style. Teddy Boys influenced both mods and rockers as well as punks – many of these subcultures would influence the goth movement, as we will see later. They were mocked for their extravagant, vintage look, as are goths and other subcultures today, but they were rebelling against the strict conformity, class boundaries and, in many cases, the dreary limitations of life in post-war Britain.

Beatniks were student rebels in the United States. They went against the mainstream aesthetic of the 1950s, which was big skirts, soft colours and femininity for women and formal suits for men. While goths tend to be over the top and Beatniks were known for being pared back, they did share some

As the 1960s approached, more subcultures evolved, including mods, rockers and hippies.

As the 1960s approached, more subcultures evolved, including mods, rockers and hippies. The decade saw an explosion in youth culture, as teenagers rebelled against the traditional values prized by their parents. Young designers and cool boutiques popped up all over London, especially in Carnaby Street and the King's Road. Some designers, for example, Mary Quant, made clothes in the back of their shops and sold them at the front. New styles and bright colours flew off the shelves.

'Mod' was short for 'modernist'. Mods enjoyed modern jazz, R&B, and some types of rock. They saw other subcultures as being too scruffy but, while wanting to look smart and modern, they rejected the suits of previous generations as too dull. Many designed their own suits and took them to local tailors while others turned to young tailors like John Stephen (the 'King of Carnaby Street') and were inspired by the lifestyles of urban Italians and American college students featuring in popular films of the time.

Mod suits featured skinny trousers and sharp jackets. They favoured black and white, with bold shapes. For a more casual look, they wore tight jeans and smart polo tops by Fred Perry. They liked brand names, sleek shapes and having the best of everything, and many mod shops popped up on Carnaby Street to cater to them. Female mods wore mini dresses and skirts by designers such as Mary Quant. Mods rebelled by dressing in a chic, cool fashion, paying attention to their clothes in a similar way to goths, who overdress in historical formal wear as a sign of nonconformity.

stylistic similarities. For a start, there was the colour black. Beatniks opted for black or monochrome clothes, suggesting they weren't much bothered by fashion. Many of them were academics and writers, such as Jack Kerouac and Allen Ginsberg. They celebrated their brains by accessorising them; for example, the poet Hettie Jones wore her glasses proudly. Many modern-day goths have bookish leanings, and the historical influences on their clothes can reference this. The Merriam–Webster Dictionary gives the broad definition of a beatnik as 'a usually young and artistic person who rejects the mores of conventional society', which could just as easily be used to describe a goth.

Teenagers in the 1950s enjoyed rock and roll music, which would go on to develop into many other rock and indie genres, including goth rock. If it weren't for rock and roll bands there would probably be no goth bands. Rock and roll music took its origins from African-American soul music. Some bands and performers of the 1950s had darker tendencies that, in retrospect, sowed the seeds for goth rock, punk rock and other types of more subversive guitar music, including acts such as Screaming Lord Sutch, who wore a top hat and white face paint, and Screamin' Jay Hawkins, who recorded the first version of *I Put a Spell on You*.

Hippie or goth? Both subcultures
have links to paganism and magic.

The rockers, who at the time were known as leather boys or ton-up boys, rode motorbikes instead of mopeds and dressed like American bikers, in jeans, boots and leather jackets, often customised and intentionally damaged, as inspired by Marlon Brandon in the banned 1953 film *The Wild Ones*. This remains the uniform of many punks, rockers, grungers and even goths (in darker colours). It has become an easy sartorial language with which to convey rebellion. Costume designers will often use torn jeans or leather jackets to represent the rebel or the bad boy. By emulating Americans and wearing what had once been workwear or practical wear, at a time when many bars, clubs, workplaces and restaurants were still implementing strict dress codes, the rockers were rebelling and setting an anti-establishment template.

Both mods and rockers influenced modern-day goth culture – the mods with their attention to and care of their clothes and the wearing of suits and the desire to make formal wear cool, and the rockers with their alternative lifestyles, tastes in music, leather jackets and boots.

One of the most famous subcultures that has stood the test of time is the hippie movement of the 1960s. Its influence of goths may seem surprising, as hippies are often known for bright colours and floral prints; indeed, punks and some goths were openly hostile towards hippies. This has changed, however, in the twenty-first century.

Hippies favoured clothes inspired loosely by the medieval period, including flowing sleeves, long skirts and loose dresses. Many hippie clothes simply need to be dyed black to suddenly appear very gothic. The floral psychedelic prints were inspired by Victorian fabrics and the work of designers like William Morris, with the colours turned up a notch. If turned down, on the other hand, they appear gothic. Both goth and hippie subcultures also count witches and Wiccans amongst their number.

Whilst some subcultures come and go, it can be argued that they also morph and evolve into other groups. There have always been people who favour dramatic clothes, a sense of individuality and an interest in counterculture, so while goths as we know them today were yet to be established at this point, other subcultures were laying the groundwork for their arrival later in the century.

As the 1970s approached, more subcultures started to appear and, in retrospect, we know that the goths were in sight. Subcultures are heavily linked to the music they listen to. Some music scholars have tried to pinpoint when (modern) goths actually appeared on the scene; although the term 'goth' had not been coined or recognised in the sense of a subculture in the 1970s, some bands began creating rock music with a darker undertone, which many now consider to have been heavily influential in establishing the goth scene.

In the 1970s, rock was a firmly established mainstream genre, so the next generation of teenagers needed to develop their own musical style and rebel against it. Previously, whilst promoting subversion against the mainstream, subcultures such as the Teddy Boys still adopted masculine archetypes. However,

glam rockers and punks experimented openly with gender and sex. Glam rock stars, mostly men, dressed flamboyantly, reminiscent – to this author's eyes, at least – of the macaronis of the 1700s crossed with sci-fi characters. David Bowie was counted among them and would later go on to attract a large goth cult following after playing the Goblin King in the film *Labyrinth* (1986).

The Marble Index, released in 1969 by Nico, is often credited with being an early goth album, although nobody knew that on its release. It has a dark, folksy feel, conjuring up images of ancient witches' and priestesses' incantations. Retrospectively, her relationship with Jim Morrison has been seen as a big influence on the album. Jim Morrison and his band The Doors are often described as early pre-goths. The Velvet Underground are also considered proto-goths, especially on their joint album with Nico, *The Velvet Underground & Nico* (1967). The band also started out dressing entirely in black.

The glam rockers of the 1970s were a reaction against the hippie music of the 1960s. The clothes were purposely androgynous and included feathers, spandex, face paint and big hair. Whereas the hippies rejected make-up and hair products in going for a natural look as an act of rebellion, both glam rockers and punks (and, subsequently, goths) went for the opposite approach, using make-up and hairstyling along with costume-like clothes to rebel and mark themselves as different from the norm. Glam rockers also wore platform boots, which bear more than a

Gene Simmons of KISS.

passing resemblance to the New Rock boot favoured by modern goths (New Rock specialises in big, chunky black boots adorned with buckles).

Wizzard were fronted by Roy Wood, his proto-goth appearance being somewhat at odds with their upbeat, cheesy songs, such as *See My Baby Jive* and *I Wish it Could be Christmas Everyday* (both 1973). Wood was famous for his pale face make-up, decorated with stars, exaggeratedly blackened eyes and back-combed hair.

Alice Cooper (originally the name of the band until its break-up, after which frontman Vincent Furnier legally adopted it) was part of the 1970s rock scene. Sporting long tangled black hair and heavily made-up eyes, he pioneered shock rock – which involved wild theatrics on stage, including fake blood, snakes and weapons. The shock rock genre has influenced many later goth performers and rock bands (such as Slipknot and Marilyn Manson), and the name Alice Cooper has become – along with Morticia – a byword to describe a goth.

KISS is another glam rock band with a goth aesthetic. Their camp look is a theatrical, exaggerated version of goth, which nonetheless influences the public perception of goths, with their black and metallic clothes, white faces, black eyes and red lips.

The 1970s musical *The Rocky Horror Picture Show* was inspired by B-movies and experimented with gender, with male cast members wearing lingerie and make-up.

Punks had a reputation for violence and chaos; their clothes weren't always expensive but they spent

The Cure, 1984, Fin Costello/Redferns.

fashion and music. Westwood and Jordan favoured dark lipstick and heavy eye make-up, along with using underwear as outerwear and celebrating items such as stockings and suspenders. As well as still being associated with punks, these are also now very much park of the goth wardrobe.

Punks enjoyed radical hairstyles, dying their hair different colours and spiking it up. In 1976, the British band The Sex Pistols burst onto the scene with their attention-grabbing sound. Their manager, Malcolm McLaren, was Vivienne Westwood's partner, so punks were associated with fashion from the very beginning. They did not wear black exclusively, but it featured heavily in their wardrobes, as did boots, leather, studs and fishnet tights. Their music was fast, frantic, aggressive-sounding and full of taboo language. Punks experimented widely with piercings and tattoos. Whilst they have now become mainstream, their behaviour was shocking at the time, and they were probably the best-known British subculture to create such controversy.

Some 1970s bands on the punk scene have since been acknowledged as goth or, at least, as having laid the foundations for the movement. The Damned have a gothic-sounding name and an equally gothic frontman, ex-gravedigger Dave Vanian. He was a poster boy for goth style, with his black T-shirts, frilly shirts and leather jackets, teamed with his dark hair and pale skin and topped off with a Dracula-style cape.

Joy Division formed in 1976, and whilst not outwardly goth in their appearance, they are

a lot of time and energy making them look ripped, well-worn and homemade. Fetish fashion, with PVC rubber, straps and lacings, was also a big influence on the punk scene, because it was seen as taboo. They also adopted the Doc Marten boot, originally designed as workwear by Griggs, the British family cobblers, who adapted the German Klaus Märtens's air-cushioned sole. They quickly became the preferred footwear of punks, followed by goths and many other alternative fashion tribes.

One of the fashion innovators of the punk scene was Vivienne Westwood. She founded the SEX boutique on the King's Road; partly inspired by 1950s fetish, it was intended to shock – and it did. One of its most famous faces was the shop assistant and stylist Jordan (real name Pamela Rooke). SEX served as a meeting place for those willing to experiment with

Siouxsie Sioux, 1979,
Fin Costello/Redferns.

often credited as being the first band to have their melancholic sound described as gothic. A group of school friends formed The Cure, and frontman Robert Smith has maintained a very gothic look – although the band denies they are intentionally gothic. Smith has the tangled black hair, eyeliner, lipstick and black clothes that many goth boys and girls aspire to. Another goth icon who insists they are not actually a goth is Siouxsie Sioux of Siouxsie and the Banshees. Very much part of the early punk scene, Siouxsie attracted attention due to her gender and her striking bondage-inspired outfits. Her angular face, spiky black hair and dramatic make-up all had girls quickly copying her style, first of all punks, but increasingly, goths.

The Cramps wore fetish-inspired costumes and dark make-up on stage. In 1977, the Misfits set out to perform punk rock with a horror-inspired edge, known as devil rock, and later, horror punk. Like The Damned, they dressed in a punk style with an even darker edge – all black, intentionally pale make-up, spiked hair and dark eyes, resembling characters from a horror film. Their skull logo, known as the 'Fiend Skull', features heavily on their merchandise to this day, and features in plenty of goth wardrobes.

In 1979, Bauhaus released the ultimate goth anthem, the epic and haunting *Bela Lugosi's Dead*. Whilst the idea and look of punk still exists and resonates today, many music scholars argue that true punk only had only a brief lifespan during the mid-1970s. Chaotic and frantic as it was, punk music splintered into many ever-evolving niches, making rock music the varied genre it is today. It did not take long for music journalists to start trying to work out what was rising from the ashes of punk in the early 1980s. The styles included New Romantics, post punk, New Wave and those who were trying to do something both gloomy and theatrical with what punk had left behind. Music journalists decided to call these people goths.

1980s to the Present Day

Modern Goths

⸻ ◆◆ ⸻

The late twentieth century saw the birth of the modern-day goth, and the gothic scene has been evolving ever since. There have been different eras of goths: the 1980s Batcave goths, the industrial goths of the 1990s, the sensitive emos of the 2000s, the vintage-inspired rockabillies, as well as the Victorian-influenced steampunks, Japanese gothic Lolita and the futuristic cybergoths. The 2010s saw the explosion of social media, providing increased exposure to existing gothic tribes and allowing new ones to flourish.

As we saw in the previous chapter, some of the punk and rock music of the previous decade has been described as gothic; as the 1980s dawned, the term was shortened to simply goth. It was popularised by music journalists. Goths themselves were less keen to embrace the new term, not wishing to be pigeonholed.

In 1982, the goth nightclub Batcave operated on Wednesdays, based at the Gargoyle nightclub in London. It became synonymous with the movement. Goths would dress up (or 'goth up') in their dark attire and go there to dance and meet like-minded people. While the Batcave no longer exists, the term 'Batcaver' is still sometimes used to describe the original 1980s goths.

The New Romantics are closely related to goths, with their love of historical flourishes and dramatic clothing. Some punks became goths; others became New Romantics (like Adam Ant); others just stayed punk. Vivienne Westwood was among the punks who embraced the historical aesthetic with her *Pirates* collection, which helped propel her from punk boutique owner and stylist to fashion royalty.

Even mainstream fashion in the 1980s was very extravagant, referencing historical styles, especially Victorian, but also the 1940s and 1950s. The wedding dress industry exploded in this decade after the seemingly fairy-tale wedding of Lady Diana Spencer and Prince Charles; the whole world

Woman wearing a gothic gown in gothic surroundings.

was awed by her Elizabeth Emanuel gown and proceeded to imitate its puffed sleeves and skirts.

In the 1980s, fans of goth music dressed like glamorous, black-wearing punks. As the scene evolved in the 1980s, bands became more consciously goth and played up to a dark costume aesthetic, incorporating more elements of historical dress, fetish and fabrics, such as lace and velvet.

Elements often associated with a 1980s goth wardrobe included fishnet tights, black jeans, spiked or messy hair, leather jackets, fingerless lace gloves and visible lingerie. Some of these elements also appeared in punk and New Romantic fashion, but the key difference was that goths tended to dress in all black. Make-up also made goths stand out, especially black and dark lipstick, pale skin and heavy dramatic eye make-up. Like punks, goth hair was often dyed and spiked extremely high, making for a striking profile.

It is generally agreed that the goth scene started in London. Whereas in the UK early goth music resembles gloomy punk or indie music, in America, it tended to be more theatrical, heavier and glam rock–influenced, eventually evolving into death metal, horror punk and shock rock.

GOTH MUSIC

Whilst some of the earlier punk and New Wave bands with a gothic sound or look, such as Siouxsie and the Banshees, The Damned and The Cure, continued to make music in the 1980s, other bands came to the fore, including The Sisters of Mercy, from Leeds. Their line-up changed several times, but they generally wore dark leather jackets, glasses and sometimes even top hats. One of their long-time members, Patricia Morrison, later joined The Damned and married the vampiric Dave Vanian. Morrison was a 1980s goth fashion pioneer. Her long dark hair and fashion sense influenced the first generation of goth women (and men). To this day, her image is still a defining goth look, and Sisters of Mercy T-shirts are widely worn by goths. The only remaining original band member Andrew Eldritch is the template for male goth style with his dark clothes and glasses.

Members of the band Specimen experimented with cross-dressing by wearing make-up, fishnet tights, artfully ragged clothes, leather and crosses, along with mohawk hair.

Death rock was a style that emerged from the American punk scene. Like the punks before them, they incorporated elements with a shock factor into their dress, including Roman Catholic symbols such as rosary beads. Christian Death's frontman Rozz Williams cross-dressed and wore a crown of thorns along with heavy goth-style make-up.

In the early 1980s, some bands were uncomfortable at being labelled 'goth', but as the decade progressed, bands began to experiment with darker looks and sounds, including shocking or disturbing imagery and themes. Some had a harsher, 'thrash' sound, with screamed lyrics and heavy beats. Religious, especially Roman Catholic, imagery was incorporated into gothic fashion, and images began

Dave Vanian of The Damned, Ian Dickson.

performed in striking gothic outfits, including leather bodices and coats.

The influence of horror on music continued to grow, and bands in the US and Scandinavia embraced it as part of their look. The Finnish band Lordi was one of the most commercially famous, even winning the Eurovision song contest wearing monster masks and fantasy- and horror-inspired costumes in their performance, looking as if they had just stepped off a film set.

In 1989, one of the most famous faces in the world of gothic emerged, Marilyn Manson. In recent years, he has been the subject of abuse accusations, but previously, his name, face and shocking performances had come to define for mainstream media what a goth should be – although many actual goths would not agree with this.

Industrial dance music came into being in the late 1980s; unlike other forms of dance music, its angst appealed to goths. As youth culture turned towards raves as the 1990s dawned, goth culture was not to be left behind, and goth costume began to explore rivethead and cybergoth looks. Both took elements of rave-scene fashion and made them their own. In the EBM/electro/industrial-music scene, which was big in Germany and Belgium, clothes worn included T-shirts, army boots and, for women, fetish-inspired looks, with rivetheads tending to be more masculine. These fashions were also inspired by heavy industrial-style clothing, including heavy-duty boots, combat trousers and metal spikes.

to appear on T-shirts and accessories associated with horror films, such as blood and bones or devils. This continues to this day.

The heavier styles of thrash, death metal and death rock all continued to emerge through the 1980s and 1990s, especially in America. Bands mostly featured male line-ups, sporting long hair, dark, artfully messy clothes and tattoos. These included bands such as Metallica and Slayer.

By the early 1990s, Scandinavian death metal had evolved as a genre in its own right. Once again, the mostly male performers sported heavy goth make-up, wore black leather and denim and used Christian images (such as crosses) in controversial ways (upside down). There were a few female band members, such as Floor Jansen of Nightwish, who

Cybergoths and cyberpunks mixed the bright colours of the rave scene with black clothes, and tended to experiment with sci-fi or futurist influences, such as goggles, masks and tubing, synthetic fabrics and brightly coloured hair, often in a dreadlock style.

Grunge music also became popular in the 1990s; its look was ripped baggy jeans, plaid shirts and T-shirts, which also could be incorporated into gothic fashion.

The 2000s saw the emo scene bloom. Emos listened to very moody, emotional rock music and wore tight black jeans, hoodies, striped T-shirts or T-shirts with skeleton or broken-heart imagery. Heavily made-up eyes were popular, as was long straight hair swept across the forehead. They saw themselves as a newer, softer type of teenager more in touch with their emotions, and, if the tabloids are to be believed, were at higher risk of self-harm and suicide. They embraced the androgynous nature of the gothic scene by not being ashamed of being in touch with their emotions – something which chimed with a lot of new thinking in the twenty-first century.

Various forms of rock and indie music also continued to be popular in the 2000s. The early part of the decade saw the scruffy elements of grunge lingering in alternative fashions, including grebos, who wore baggy clothes, lots of jewellery and elements of gothic fashion, and listened to rock music. (Before the explosion of the internet, some subcultures had names in local dialect as well, for example in Bristol, 'jitter' was used as a word for grebo.) The

practice of mixing more formal items such as blazers and waistcoats with T-shirts was adopted widely both in mainstream fashion and subculture. Skateboarding also became popular with teenagers, and skaters tended to be associated with baggy jeans and chunky trainers such as Vans. Many subcultures, including goths, adopted extremely baggy trousers in the early to mid-2000s. Steampunk also began to grow in popularity.

Some Western music genres became popular in Japan, such as death rock. A style of Japanese rock music evolved in the 1990s called visual kei, which focused on extreme costumes and became important to the Japanese goth scene.

Many singers in goth rock bands add an element of opera to their music – not only for its tragic associations but also for the pomp and theatricality. This is often missed by the mainstream: while goths dress in black and perhaps look depressed, much of this is a performance – goths at heart love the theatricality of dress, music and story. Operatic-infused goth musicians include Evanescence's lead singer Amy Lee, and Diamanda Galás, whose experimental music addresses social themes and whose elegant, long black dresses and long black hair combine to produce a stunning, sultry gothic look.

The female-led group Miranda Sex Garden mixed rock music with medieval choral sounds; some of its members went on to form the Mediæval Bæbes, a successful 1990s group which used a girl-band format to release classical medieval music, often wearing beautiful medieval-inspired ballgowns; while on first listen, their sound might not resemble contemporary goth music, they were certainly performing historically gothic music, and their look was very appealing and aspirational to goths of both genders.

Sharon den Adel of the Dutch band Within Temptation is known for her dramatic gothic costumes which she designs herself, and her beautiful voice. Her accompanying theatrical rock band deny they are related to the gothic, but they could be categorised as metal or symphonic rock.

Through the 1980s and 1990s, dream pop emerged from the post-punk scene: dream-like, ethereal music which included bands such as Cranes, This Mortal Coil and My Bloody Valentine. This type of music appeals to both goths and hippies. This may have seemed odd, given the enmity between punks and hippies, but as the gothic scene expanded to incorporate other elements of culture beyond music, including folklore, links with certain elements of hippie culture became more apparent. This also showed itself in 1990s gothic fashion, with a move towards more crushed velvets and flowing sleeves.

Goth vibes travelled across to Australia and New Zealand. Nick Cave, an iconic Australian goth musician whose music combines the blues with brooding rock music, moved to the UK in the 1980s. His band The Bad Seeds has earned him the nickname the Prince of Darkness, even though he has also parodied the goth genre with the song 'Release the Bats'. Susie Cave, his wife, has her own line of luxurious vintage-inspired dresses and jewellery, The Vampire's Wife.

Between the 1980s and today, many other goth subcultures have emerged with no links to music at all, such as Victorian-style goths or pastel goths. The subculture has become much more about fashion and lifestyle, such as Wiccan beliefs or an interest in gothic novels. However, many goth festivals and iconic clubs continue to appear: what better way to show off your fashion? Interestingly for a scene that famously attracts introverts, with many goths not wishing to draw attention to themselves, they are quite a brilliant sight.

CLUBS AND FESTIVALS

The most important club night in the history of goths is the previously mentioned Batcave, which has changed venue a few times but remained in central London. Slimelight and KitKat were other well-known London goth nights. KitKat took its name from an eighteenth-century gentleman's society, as did the Hellfire Club, a goth club in New York which was established in 1983.

Other cities had their own goth and alternative clubs, including Bar Phono in Leeds and the Bristol Bierkeller; Oslo had Gotham Nights. Through the 1990s, goth club nights continued to grow – often located in bigger clubs which would provide a variety of alternative nights and events, targeted at different subcultures. They were often in cities with large student populations, such as the Wendy House club night in Leeds, Batfink in Sheffield and Resurgence in Portsmouth.

Whitby Goth Weekend,
photograph by Gary Platt.

Goth nights in the 2010s often mentioned 'circus' or 'ball' in the title to encourage certain dress codes, appealing to more historically influenced goths who would jump at the chance to don a ballgown or tailcoat. One such event was Dark Circus Party in Bloomsbury in London, which encouraged very theatrical ball-inspired dress, with burlesque performances, music and suitably gothic themes. After midnight, more fetish fans would emerge.

Goth night clubs have spread across the world, often functioning as fashion shows for goths to parade their styles in the days before Instagram. Sometimes they are nightclubs in their own right, and sometimes they are goth nights hosted by the local alternative clubs. Such nights can be inspiring and provide a sense of community – quite rare if you are a goth!

By the 1990s, festivals were becoming more commonplace and more accessible for all sorts of genres of music and interests. Goth was no exception. The most well known of the goth festivals is the Whitby Goth Weekend, started in 1994 by Jo Hampshire, who received so much interest from her advert looking for Goth pen pals, she organised a meet-up in Whitby.

Whitby has a very special gothic significance; it was one of the settings of Bram Stoker's *Dracula*, and Whitby Abbey sits in ruins on a cliff surrounded by the cemetery of St Mary's church. This historic fishing town has the North Sea on one side – next stop the North Pole – and the wide expanse of the North York Moors on the other. Even today, it is very difficult to access without a car, its isolation adding to the gothic splendour

of this pretty Victorian town. Whitby is known for producing Whitby jet, a black stone used especially in mourning jewellery, and now, goth jewellery. Whitby's whalebone arch commemorates its whaling history.

The meet-up that Jo Hampshire organised soon put Whitby on the alternative fashion map. Twice a year, in April and October, goths descend on the town dressed in their finest to mix and mingle. Goth music, goth markets and goth film screenings are organised and photographers from the world's press capture photographs of goths in all their finery.

The Wave-Gotik-Treffen goth festival in Germany features a Victorian gothic picnic, and attendees sport an array of historically influenced Goth costumes. M'era Luna is another festival based in Germany. Goth fashions and lifestyle influenced by the Middle Ages have become very popular amongst German youth.

Wave-Gotik-Treffen, photograph by Martin Soulstealer.

Bats Day in the Fun Park takes over Disneyland in California for the day, evidence that goth has reached family-friendly audiences and continues to be popular in the United States and Canada. Other American goth festivals include Convergence and Drop Dead, which began at the CBCG club in New York but has also been held in European cities.

As well as these contemporary festivals, older festivals have become intertwined within goth subculture. Halloween is the most obvious of these, the festival in which everyone 'goes goth' for a day. The festival has roots in ancient Celtic society and was thought to be the time when ghosts and fairies would cross over into the mortal realm, made easier by the dark and cold autumnal nights. To combat this, the Celts made bonfires, wore masks and left out 'soul' cakes to ward away evil spirits. This was especially important as this scary time coincided with the harvest and with the ancient Celtic festival of Samhain.

When the Romans conquered the Celtic lands, they appropriated their festivals, tying Samhain with Feralia, a festival honouring the dead and the goddess Pomona, the goddess of fruit trees, gardens and orchards (this is possibly how apples came to be linked with Halloween).

It was then Christianity's turn to incorporate this now popular festival. All Souls' Day and All Saints' Day were moved to early November to tie in with the festivities, a time to mark and honour those who had already passed on. The festival was still widely celebrated by the Irish when they emigrated to America en masse after the Irish Potato Famine, and they took these traditions with them. This included carving scary faces into turnips and leaving them outside their doors to keep away the damned soul of Stingy Jack. The easier availability of the pumpkin in America made it the vegetable of choice; its orange colour can be associated with Halloween thanks to the bonfires and autumn leaves. Native Americans were thought to have added storytelling around the fire to the proceedings.

With the increase in commercialisation and growing disbelief in superstitions of the twentieth century, the festival began to be celebrated widely in America, with children dressing up in homemade or store-bought costumes and tricking or treating. This was linked to both the soul cakes tradition and the Scottish tradition of guising, in which children took on the role of ghosts who were offered food in exchange for staying away from the house.

Halloween costumes tend to involve dressing as a scary creature. Bedsheets were used to represent burial shrouds. Halloween parades took place from the 1920s. By the 1950s, Halloween had become enshrined in popular culture, while the slasher movies of the late 1970s and early 1980s added to its scary mythology. Halloween is now big business, with home decorations and Halloween-themed food, and many popular TV shows producing Halloween specials.

Costumes have become increasingly sexy, as adults and university students now also celebrate Halloween. They also tend to go beyond simply

Day of the Dead–style make-up.

scary, and sometimes reference a public figure whose skeletons in the closet have been revealed.

The Day of the Dead festival is often confused with Halloween. Originally celebrated in Mexico, it has now spread to many other countries. Similarly to Halloween, it began with an ancient people – in this case, the Aztecs – honouring their goddess Mictēcacihuātl, the lady of the dead, who ruled the underworld with her husband Mictlāntēcutli. She is often shown as a skeleton, or wearing a skirt made of snakes. As well as watching over the dead, she also swallowed the stars in her huge jaws to allow the Day of the Dead to happen.

As with Samhain, the conquering Spanish gave this festival a Christian meaning, as a time to honour the dead. Children return from the dead on November 1st; adults on the 2nd. Carnival-style celebrations also take place, with many participants painting their faces like skulls and wearing golden marigolds in their hair. The bright colours of the marigolds are thought to help guide spirits. The cartoons of José Guadalupe Posada have popularised specifically Mexican-looking skulls. Sugar skulls are left as offerings for the dead and are mimicked worldwide as face paint.

The resurgence of the popularity of Frida Kahlo has added to the international interest in the Day of the Dead, while gothic fashion has embraced the skulls and flower crowns of Mexican culture. Skulls have long featured in gothic aesthetics, from designer Alexander McQueen to the films of Tim Burton to Victorian memento moris.

Overleaf: Young gothic women wearing headdresses that mix roses with crowns, attending the annual costume ball Gala Nocturna in Ghent, March 2016, photographed by Martin Soulstealer. The headdresses in the pictures give the look of a Catholic saint or an ancient queen. More elaborate headdresses including these elements have become increasing popular in 2020s gothic fashion as images of powerful historical women, whether they be saints, queens or pagan goddesses are uncovered, explored, reclaimed and celebrated.

Another form of nightlife which attracts goths is the burlesque scene. Growing in popularity in the 1990s and then erupting in the 2000s and 2010s, the style was a revival and modernisation of the burlesque and cabaret events popular from the nineteenth to the mid-twentieth centuries.

Many involved in this scene had been teenage goths and were now looking for a way to continue celebrating historical dress. Both goth and burlesque cultures celebrate femininity and dressing up, as well as enjoying historically inspired underwear and corsets. Rockabillies and psychobillies adopted rock-and-roll or B-movie aesthetics, which many goths already enjoyed, and made them more vintage. Both goth and burlesque cultures also enjoyed elements of circus performances and a different style of nightclub than the run-of-the-mill mainstream. Cabaret and burlesque nights now feature in many towns and cities throughout the world. Some burlesque performers strictly follow vintage styles while others may mix rockabilly aesthetic including punky, coloured hair, tattoos and piercings and a more gothic twist to their vintage clothing and accessories.

Nerdlesque and twisted burlesque are types of burlesque celebrating more freakshow elements. The celebration of fetishist elements have obvious appeal for goths, as do the historical romance aspects of well-known burlesque pin-ups, including fetishist stars such as Bettie Page and modern-day divas such as Dita von Teese. Burlesque takes the gothic and makes it glamorous and sexy.

Dita von Teese is a burlesque artist who carved out a niche for herself in the 1990s and 2000s by reviving burlesque performances and giving them a modern edge. She became a pin-up, model and designer and is well known for her impeccable vintage style. She made a point of standing out, dying her naturally blonde hair black when blonde hair has long been the preferred look of the Western fashion world, as well as opting for vintage make-up (including paler skin, dramatic red lipstick and eyeliner) over contemporary faux-natural looks.

Burlesque, Twin Peak Festival UK, featuring The Double R Club,
London, September 2018, Martin Soulstealer.

GOTH GOES POP CULTURE

Films

The 1980s saw a range of slasher films grow in popularity and become increasingly horrific as ratings and censorship relaxed, such as *A Nightmare on Elm Street, Silence of the Lambs* and *Scream*. The 1980s and 1990s saw remakes of several of the original gothic horror films and retellings of earlier horror characters, sometimes making vampires and witches more sympathetic.

Popular additions to the vampire genre included *The Lost Boys* (1987), in which vampires are given leather jackets and a punky look, and *The Hunger* (1983), featuring David Bowie sporting sunglasses and a slick, contemporary suit on the film poster. *Dracula* was reprised and played by Gary Oldman in 1992. *Interview with the Vampire* (1994) was hugely successful and featured two 1990s Hollywood hunks as vampires – Tom Cruise as a villainous vampire and Brad Pitt filled with regret – their stories charted through history with a range of fantastical costumes. *Blade* (1998) took vampire films into more action-adventure territory and starred Wesley Snipes, an African-American actor, as the half-vampire lead, sporting a long black leather coat.

The *Twilight* films, based on the books by Stephenie Meyer, were hugely successful in the 2010s; the lead vampire was a moody romantic love interest for a mortal girl, spawning a host of imitations – girl falls in love with mythical being and difficulties ensue. The *Twilight* films featured low-key, run-of-the-mill contemporary fashion: an unusual statement for a vampire movie, but perhaps more approachable for a mainstream audience.

Werewolves have also featured on the big screen, from *A Company of Wolves* in 1984 to Jack Nicholson in *Wolf* in 1994. *The Mummy* also made a comeback in the late 1990s through to the 2000s, when a remake staring Brendan Fraser launched an entire franchise.

Witches are now often portrayed as good (or, at least, misunderstood) rather than bad, as the history of witchcraft takes on feminist connotations. Disney villainesses began to star in their own films, including *Cruella* and *Maleficent* (the title character played by Angelina Jolie, who already seemed quite gothic after famously pairing a black dress with a necklace that contained some of her then-partner's blood). Other films such as *Practical Magic* (1998) gave witchcraft a fun, romantic-comedy setting. The novel *Wicked*, which became a successful stage musical, tells the story of the Wizard of Oz from the point of view of the Wicked Witch of the West.

Detective fiction sprang from gothic fiction in the 1800s, and it still features gothic looks and characters, such as the novel *The Girl with the Dragon Tattoo* (2011). In films made of this modern Scandi thriller, the main character, Lisbeth Salander, dresses in a goth style.

One director whose films are forever linked with gothic visuals is Tim Burton. His works include *Beetlejuice, Frankenweenie, The Nightmare Before Christmas, Edward Scissorhands, Batman, Alice in*

Family-friendly films with horror characters and a comedic edge became hugely popular, feeding gothic ideas and stories, introducing children to gothic looks and fashion from an early age.

Wonderland, and *Sleepy Hollow.* His films tend to attract family audiences, despite their dark and macabre themes and gothic look; he is especially known for his love of stripes and top hats in his Victorian and circus-inspired costumes and sets. He often works with gothically-inclined actors, such as Winona Ryder, his ex-wife Helena Bonham Carter and Johnny Depp. Guillermo del Toro is another director known for producing films with a gothic look, such as *Pan's Labyrinth;* his films, however, are definitely not for children.

Family-friendly films with horror characters and a comedic edge became hugely popular, feeding on gothic ideas and stories, introducing children to gothic looks and fashion from an early age. Some of the most famous include *Casper the Friendly Ghost, Hocus Pocus, Coco, Hotel Transylvania* and the previously mentioned *Addams Family* remake.

Some films take futuristic and historical settings and give them a gothic edge, such as Guy Ritchie's neo-Victorian take on Sherlock Holmes, which has a very steampunk feel, and *The Matrix* – which went on to inspire cyberpunks – famous for its long black coats, leather and the gothic theme of a young man out of place.

Magazines, Comics and Graphic Novels

The 1980s and early 2000s saw a flurry of gothic magazines, but with the rise of the internet these gradually faded out, until only a few remain. Some have been reincarnated as websites and Instagram sites, now the most common way to view new gothic looks.

Censorship on comic books was relaxed in the 1970s, meaning gothic and horror themes could be featured more explicitly. Some of the most famous examples include *From Hell* by Alan Moore (featuring Jack the Ripper) and *The Sandman* by Neil Gaiman. The goth cartoon strip *Nemi* featured in national newspapers such as the *Metro*, and the likenesses of goth cartoon characters such as Emily Strange are mass-produced and merchandised, and sold in a variety of outlets.

Books

Horror-genre books also became more popular. Splatter punk was big in the 1980s, and the 1990s saw the *Point Horror* and *Goosebumps* series, aimed at teen and pre-teen audiences, respectively. Stephen King, one of the most successful horror writers of all time, was also going from strength to strength. The *Twilight* saga made the 'sad mythical boy in love' genre even more popular in books than it had been in films.

Throughout the 1980s and 1990s, witches went from being wholly evil to aspirational, magical characters popular with children; *The Worst Witch* and *Harry Potter* influenced a whole generation of children, persuading them that witches were good.

Much gothic fiction is now child-friendly, such as the work of Marcus Sedgwick and the *Goth Girl* series by Chris Riddell. Other heavily illustrated gothic books include *Lemony Snicket's A Series of Unfortunate Events,* and Holly Black and Tony DiTerlizzi's *The Spiderwick Chronicles.* Children now grow up with

gothic imagery – which no longer always has negative connotations – firmly installed in their imagination.

Dystopian and fantasy genres for adults and young adults have increased in popularity in the twenty-first century, along with a craze for Victorian settings and sets, such as circuses and freak shows, all drawing on gothic elements.

TV

The trends that have been seen in publishing and film have also been apparent on TV; in the same way, the easing of censorship has allowed horror to become more horrific, although horror characters are now often painted in a more sympathetic and comedic light, as new ways have been discovered to tell old stories. Rampaging dystopian zombies, romantic vampires and smart witches reign supreme here as well, with TV programmes such as *The Walking Dead, Being Human, Ghosts, Sabrina the Teenage Witch* and *American Horror Story.*

Buffy the Vampire Slayer was a huge hit in the late 1990s and early 2000s; it took several classical horror types such as vampires, witches and werewolves, sometimes painting them in a more positive or sexy light. Detective stories – especially Victorian-based ones such as *Sherlock Holmes* – have received several retellings, while shows such as *Penny Dreadful* fuse fantasy, horror and detective stories in a gothic Victorian setting.

Other TV shows feature gothic characters as a type – the surreal comedy *The Mighty Boosh* launched the career of goth alternative comedian Noel Fielding, who also played a goth character in *The IT Crowd*. Other goth comedians include Russell Brand and Tim Minchin. Goth is arguably much less feared than it used to be, with Noel Fielding even presenting *The Great British Bake Off*. The comedy film *What We Do In The Shadows*, which sent up vampiric stereotypes, has now been converted into a successful TV series in which several of the characters are dressed in very over-the-top gothic vampiric style for comedic value.

Serious shows which feature goth characters include NCIS; although Abby Sciuto is a forensic office – and, so, works regularly with the dead(!) – she is an upbeat character, and the show is not about the supernatural. Soap operas such as *Home and Away* and *Coronation Street* have also included goth characters.

Elvira (played by Cassandra Peterson) was the hostess of the TV show *Elvira's Movie Macabre*. She dressed in revealing gothic attire, famously including a low-cut black dress with a slit up the leg. Her camp, gothic persona proved so successful that as well as hosting the show from 1981–86, she has also written and appeared in Elvira movies, as well as featuring in a range of magazines and comics, appearing in adverts and making public appearances at events.

Many pop stars such as Rihanna and Christina Aguilera have also experimented with goth looks. It is an easy way to signal rebellion and although it has gone through periods of being 'cool', it has still never been mainstream fashion.

FASHION FROM THE HIGH STREET TO THE CATWALK

Nowadays, goth can be found on the high street. It is an easy byword for looks as wide-ranging as rebellion and dark glamour. Every few years, in their autumn or winter issues, fashion magazines such as *Vogue* do fashion shoots inspired by goth fashion, and high street shops release winter ranges with a gothic edge. *Gothic: Dark Glamour* was an exhibition at the FIT (Fashion Institute of Technology) NYC in 2008, featuring designers, film costumes and historical costumes.

The rise of fast fashion has made clothes cheaper for many, so, while some goths still seek out their town's goth shop or market stall, many now turn to the high street or cheaper online retailers. Many high street shops cheaply recreate a variety of looks, whereas, historically, goth shops were often expensive for a teen budget. The greater availability of cheaper clothes may explain why people today do not necessarily stick with one subculture, but go through several looks and lifestyles or blend various styles. However, fast fashion has impacted negatively on the environment, so the early 2020s have seen much discussion about a return to slower and, therefore, probably more expensive fashion.

Many designers dabble in gothic, that is, the subculture that celebrates fashion. Many will stage a goth-inspired catwalk show at some point, especially for their autumn and winter collections.

Alexander McQueen was a notable designer who used gothic fashion for inspiration. He originally

Alexander McQueen Autumn/Winter 2013, Bukajlo Frederic.

designed for Givenchy and also worked with jewellery designer Shaun Leane. McQueen's designs have long been associated with the goth look; his corsets resembling the human body bring to mind *Frankenstein*. Originally training as a tailor, he moved on to make bold fashion statements, with explicitly gothic collections such as *Jack the Ripper Stalks His Victims* and *Highland Rape*. McQueen's 2015 exhibition at the V&A was a sellout, with many of the rooms transformed into gothic settings to best showcase his work.

The fashionista Isabella Blow originally discovered McQueen. She worked as a fashion editor and wore a variety of striking styles, many with a gothic flavour. An exhibition of her wardrobe was held at Somerset House, showing off her fabulous theatrical style to its full potential.

Another famous gothic muse and model, Daphne Guinness, embraced the white streak in her hair; she is frequently photographed wearing a variety of gothic designs.

Vivienne Westwood's designs often draw on elements of British history, as well as folklore. Some of her collections which appeal to goths include: *Pirates* (Autumn/Winter 1981/2); *Nostalgia of Mud* (autumn/winter 82/83); *Witches* (autumn/winter 1983/4); *Mini Crini* (spring/summer 1985); *Harris Tweed* 1987/8; *Pagani* (spring/summer 1988); *Portrait* (autumn/winter 1990/1); *Dressing Up* (autumn/winter 1991/2); *Anglomania* (autumn/winter 1993/4); *Café Society* (spring/summer 1994); *Vive La Cocotte* (autumn/winter 1995/6);

Vivienne Westwood Fall/Winter 1995 (Vive la Cocotte),
Gérard Julien.

Daphne Guinness.

Les Femmes (spring/summer 1996); and *Wild Beauty* (autumn/winter 2001/2). As is evident in some of the names of these collections, they were strongly inspired by historical fashions, especially from the eighteenth and nineteenth centuries. Corsets, full skirts, layering, crinolines, long coats and structured tailoring are all signatures of Westwood's designs, and are also favoured by gothic fashionistas.

Designer Pam Hogg arose from the punk scene and is still going strong. Her designs reference punk, historicism and fetish wear. Zandra Rhodes is another British designer whose designs reference punk, but often interpreted in a fairy-tale way — making punk pretty. She has designed many gowns that would appeal to both goths and punks.

The American designer Anna Sui explores various subcultures and eras. Many of her styles and collections have gothic elements, especially her 1994 and 2013 spring collections (which drew heavily on punk), her 1993 spring collection (grunge), her 1992, 2005 and 2007 autumn collections (1970s rock stars and William Morris), the collections of spring

Anna Sui Autumn/Winter
2020, Ovidiu Hrubaru.

Christian Lacroix's black wedding dress, Autumn/Winter, 1992, Victor Virgile.

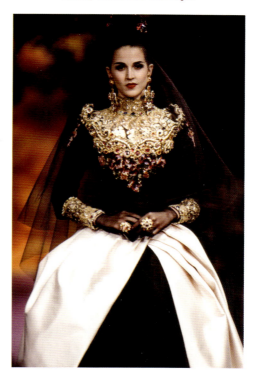

2000 and autumn 2009 (Victoriana), and her 2020 collection, which had several goth-style outfits.

Like Vivienne Westwood, the designer Christian Lacroix is heavily influenced by historical styles. The 1990s saw a range of his stunning modern princess gowns, fusing and referencing every period from medieval to Edwardian. The historic references alone can make his style look very gothic, but this is compounded by his use of dramatic colours, veils, long skirts, corsets, velvet and lace. One of the most stunning pieces was a black Renaissance-style wedding dress from his 1993 collection.

Jean Paul Gaultier references historical, retro and fetish underwear and fashion. He is favoured by Dita von Teese, who has even walked the catwalk for him. He uses bodices and corsets, as well as buckles and straps, in a fetish reference mixed with softer 1950s-style silhouettes.

Rick Owen's designs can be brutal, simplistic and androgynous, focusing on draping and otherworldliness in a style he has called 'Glunge', a mixture of glamour and and grunge – what could be more gothic? Owens founded his own successful label along with Michele Lamy, a striking gothic fashionista and his partner in both life and business. Fellow gothic designer Gareth Pugh initially worked for them and was backed by Lamy when he launched his own line. Unashamedly gothic, his inspirations are exaggerated clubwear, while his designs experiment with shape and proportion. Unsurprisingly, he also designs costumes and artwork.

Other designers who have been referred to as gothic or have described themselves as such include Ann Demeulemeester, known for her simple, chic tailoring and boho influence. Olivier Theyskens's gothic grunge designs incorporate elements of femininity. He has designed costumes for the rock band The Smashing Pumpkins and has worked for the Nina Ricci and Rocha brands. Yohji Yamamoto's gothic jewellery line of spring/summer 2020 features motifs such as skulls and top hats, while his fashion includes layering, tailoring and industrial aspects, with a post-apocalyptic and cyber feel. Experimental and avant garde designer Rei Kawakubo founded the Comme des Garçons and Dover Street Market brands and is celebrated by a range of fashionistas and subcultures alike. Andre Soriano is known for grand gothic gowns and wedding dresses.

The British goth jewellery brand Alchemy was set up in the 1970s by Geoff and Trevor Kayson Phillipson, and was one of the first companies to sell 'goth-style' jewellery: chunky, silver and inspired by Celtic designs.

The growth of 'new age' shops, primarily aimed at hippies, has increasingly appealed to goths, especially with the revival of paganism, Wicca and witchcraft from the 2010s onwards. Many of these shops, as well as selling the tools of the witch trade, also sell chunky silver jewellery, sometimes with pagan or ancient-world connections such as Egyptian symbols. Many floaty hippie clothes can suddenly look very goth in black. By the 2020s, symbols such as moons, cats and witches have become commonplace in mainstream clothing stores.

INTERNET

The rise of internet chat rooms in the 1990s kept the goth scene going and allowed it to develop a stronger identity away from music. It also allowed national and international gothic communities to connect to a far greater extent than was possible with club nights. Goths in more isolated communities could now converse with each other, and it became easier for goth ideas and looks to travel across countries.

The internet opened up a range of cheaper online retailers. Sites such as Etsy acted as virtual marketplaces for goths to sell their wares. Instagram and Pinterest are very much based on looks and aesthetics and are places to share fashions, inspiration and imagery; they feature stars who have attracted huge followings in the goth community.

GOTH FAMILIES

Original Batcave goths are now old enough to be grandparents, so gothic living has spread to all elements of life. Many mainstream toy companies such as Lego, Mattel and Playmobil have scary goth-inspired toy lines. Gothic weddings, featuring dramatic suits and wedding dresses in black and purple, are by no means commonplace but not unheard of, with historic graveyards and gothic stately homes being used as venues. Dita von Teese famously wore a purple Vivienne Westwood gown when she married Marilyn Manson.

It is now possible to buy goth-inspired baby grows and childrenswear. Companies such as Attitude also make homeware for goths, who can now stock up any time of the year, not just at Halloween. Many of these companies have grown and gained in popularity thanks to the internet, as there probably still are not enough goths around for there to be a goth version of IKEA in every town!

GOTH TRIBES

There are various categories of goth, which is one of the reasons the scene has continued to grow in popularity. It has become a byword for any subculture with dark or historical influences. It is important to also remember that, while some goths like to be strict and subscribe to certain names and descriptions for their 'type', many others reject labels and blend elements from different types. Nonconformity is part of the joy of being a goth. While some people, perhaps misfits searching for a place to belong, are actively looking to join the goth community, others act as gatekeepers, checking if someone who looks like a goth ticks all the boxes, such as movie and music tastes. Sometimes goth reacts to events in the mainstream or other subcultures and makes it its own – such as the raves and grunge movement of the 1990s. Most goths simply enjoy the macabre or dressing up; others are introverted and bookish, and so prefer the literature. While many of them do like so-called 'goth music', it is possible to dress entirely goth but never have listened to a single song by The Cure (who, ironically, don't describe themselves as goth). Dressing in a slightly fantastical way is a form of self-expression and escapism. If you don't fit in with your peers, then why keep trying?

Arguably, in the last few decades the link between goth fashion and music has weakened, for three reasons: there are now so many subsets in both music and fashion; the subculture has persisted for such a long time; and its reach is now global, expanding far beyond the radius of its founding venue, the Batcave.

Dressing in a slightly fantastical way is a form of self-expression and escapism. If you don't fit in with your peers, then why keep trying?

The following is by no means a full list of the various goth 'tribes': there are different names for different types of goths in different regions, countries and even decades. These are simply some of the most well-known examples.

Elder Goth/Batcave Goth: The originals from the 1980s. They generally wear black jeans, T-shirts, shirts, dresses, leather jackets and skirts, teamed with heavy eye make-up and big hair. Many goths have some elements of the elder/original goth in their wardrobe.

Rivethead/Industrial: This look is linked to music associated with the goth scene bbecoming heavier and more industrial, so the dress is influenced by workwear, military wear, rave wear and fetish wear. Heavy fabrics such as leather and denim are also associated with this look. Heavy boots, fishnets and miniskirts are worn. There is also an element of electronic music.

Cybergoth girl.

Cyberpunks and **cybergoths** tend to wear futuristic and sci-fi–inspired rave wear. Their clothes tend to be darker. The look grew out of the rave scene of the 1990s but was also an attempt to reimagine and imitate characters and outfits from cyberpunk novels (a genre of sci-fi born in the 1980s and made famous by William Gibson's 1984 *Neuromancer* novel). Other inspirations include *Blade Runner*, *Star Trek* and *The Matrix*.

Cybergoths and cyberpunks tend to wear another colour alongside black, often a neon shade. While most goths are inspired by the past, the cybergoth is inspired by the future: shorter skirts, hot pants, skimpy tops, combat trousers, string vests, fishnets, multicoloured (and often dreadlocked) hair and wired tubed accessories with big shoes. Synthetic modern materials such as PVC are widely used. The Cyberdog shop in Camden is world famous for being a key provider for this scene – even their shop feels like a rave experience.

Steampunk was inspired by another William Gibson novel, *The Difference Engine* (1990), in collaboration with Bruce Sterling. The novel is set in the nineteenth century, with the premise that technology had developed at a faster rate than occurred historically. This highlights the ongoing links between the goth scene and literature. Many other steampunk-influenced books have been published since, spawning TV series and films.

The look is Victorian, but in a sci-fi world. The dress is very Victorian-focused, with crinolines, bustles,

Steampunk couple, Steampunk Asylum, Lincoln, UK, September 2013, Martin Soulstealer.

corsets, top hats and tailcoats, but brown is often preferred to black to create a more industrial look. Circus elements include skirts which can vary in length, showing striped tights. A key motif is to incorporate faux technology, most stereotypically a clock, but also goggles, spy glasses or even wings, looking as though they have been made by nineteenth-century hands and are possibly steam-powered. It is a very creative subculture! It started as a cosplay and appeared at comic book conventions, but has since grown into a subculture in its own right. Burlesque or cabaret performers sometimes incorporate the look.

Historical goth: Many goths love a historically influenced look; many branches exist, which also cross over. A typical female-goth look is stripy tights, tutus and corsets. However, some goths go even further than these mere nods to historicism and fully embrace historical looks, such as long Victorian skirts, blouses and crinolines.

Romantic goth: This is the name for the most obviously historically influenced goth. Women will tend to have long hair and wear long skirts, frilly blouses and corsets. Men may also have long hair, frock coats, waistcoats and shirts with cravats. This can be quite a difficult look to maintain daily, so can be referenced with Victorian-inspired jewellery, accessories or with clothing such as waistcoats. The look draws many people to the goth community, especially cosplayers and history enthusiasts.

Some Victorian-style goths opt for vague influences while others try for greater accuracy. It is also important to remember that due to workplace roles and other responsibilities, not all goths can can be as fully goth as they would like to be all the time. Some goths might go for a fully historical look on special occasions or festivals but just have subtle influences in their day-to-day lives. They are also known as neo-Victorians or traditional goths (which is sometimes also used to describe an elder goth). Edwardian goths tend to be inspired by the Edwardian dandy look and the Aesthetic Movement (inspired by figures such as Oscar Wilde.) This look has grown in popularity during the 2010s and 2020s (as

mainstream fashion has also embraced a more dandyish look, with the reappearance of items such as waistcoats).

Other historical areas which provide inspiration and have their own subsets include Egyptian-, medieval-, Renaissance-, Celtic- and Norse-style goths. Kilts appear in both gothic and punk fashion as a nod to traditional Scottish and Irish wear. Ren (Renaissance) Fairs often feature stalls selling historical and gothic ware, especially in America.

Carnival goth, vintage goth, burlesque goth, gothabilly, rockabilly and **psychobilly** are inspired by nineteenth- and twentieth-century fashions. These various 'billies' tend to be more closely linked to music, with rockabillies favouring more traditional 1950s-style music while the others favour punk or gothic takes on this musical style. Their clothes are inspired by the mid-twentieth century with various punky or gothic twists, including mixing in colours such as green, purple and red, and printing skulls and bats, for example, on more traditional 1950s dresses and shirts (which would originally have featured pastel shades and floral prints). Carnival gypsy and burlesque goths are more closely linked to performance lifestyles, favouring sexier or more revealing takes on Victorian and vintage-gothic looks.

The late twentieth and early twenty-first centuries saw a nostalgia for the middle of the twentieth century. This was for a variety of reasons, including the advent of the new millennium, the 9/11 terrorist attacks and the financial crisis from 2008 onwards. People often

Gothic Lolitas,
Harajuku, Japan.

look to the past for comfort in times of crisis. As with the Teddy Boys of the 1950s, people were able to pick up cheap second-hand clothing items from the previous generation.

This vintage trend easily translated to goths, with many adopting a vintage aesthetic, especially for the workplace. Other goths adopted the vintage look but with a gothic or punk edge – taking their inspiration from 1950s rockers rather than mainstream fashion. They focused on darker colours and fabrics (such as leather), as well as wearing vintage-inspired tattoos and dramatic, overemphasised vintage make-up (for example, over-the-top cat eyes and dramatic hair colours). Tattoos and clothing tend to be inspired by old-school Americana mixed with punk and goth aesthetics, with accessories including skull hairclips or coffin-shaped handbags.

Gothic Lolita: These fashions are striking and fantastical. The wearers look almost like hyper-Victorian dolls, with elements of the cartoonish and the cute. Lolita styling has been around since the 1970s but has changed with the times. The pure Lolita look tends to feature pink and pastels, whereas gothic Lolita is its darker twin. It has roots in the music of Japanese *kei* fashion, as well as the 1990s and 2000s Japanese scene featuring outlandish street fashions. Like steampunk, its roots are in cosplay, in this case involving manga and anime characters.

The Japanese rock star Mana from the visual kei band Malice Mizer looked to French Romanticism and the Victorian era for his fashion inspiration, eventually

launching his own clothing brand Moi-même-Moitié. Elegant gothic Lolita and elegant gothic aristocrat (for men) are even more extreme versions of this fashion.

Harajuku has a world-famous experimental fashion scene, with young people being highly creative in their interpretation of subcultures. Magazines such as *FRUiTS* specialise in street-style photojournalism – featuring goth, goth-inspired, cyberpunk, steampunk and, of course, gothic Lolita.

The Lolita look has been exported all over the world but is most commonly seen at comic-book conventions. The movement even has its own periodicals.

Corporate goth: This is a goth who has an office job, so has to wear formal work attire such as suits. They

Maleficent-style horns,
Raven Kings Ball,
Glastonbury, October 2016,
Martin Soulstealer.

often still manage to incorporate gothic elements into their outfits. These are often historically influenced, including waistcoats and pencil skirts in dark colours. Due to being at work or school, some people simply cannot be goth all the time, so take real pleasure in 'gothing' up on their time off.

Magic-influenced goths: Many goths take their fashion inspiration from folklore and magic, with some practising paganism and Wicca. Some goths take their inspiration from vampiric elements of dress, such as bloodied accessories, capes and period costumes.

Horns reference demonic creatures, as historically the devil is often portrayed with horns and linked to goats, but they also can reference other mythical creatures such as fawns. The adoption of them in recent years probably initially stems from Angelina Jolie's portrayal of Maleficent, as well as fantasy YA books such as Laini Taylor's *Daughter of Smoke and Bone* which features magical characters who have both human and animal features. There has also been a mainstream resurgence of popular astrology, some of which signs (such as Aries and Taurus) feature horned animals.

Vampric goth, Danza
Della Luna, Grand
Opera House, Ghent,
November 2019,
Martin Soulstealer.

Witchy goths or **dark fairy goths** also tend to be inspired by medieval and folksy fashions but are also very much in touch with the natural world – even if they are not practising Wiccans, they may still be interested in gardening and natural remedies, which may be reflected in their dress. As discussed, they have the most in common with hippies than other types of goths. Other similar subsets include **pagan goths** as well as **ethereal goths**, who tend to be elegant and intelligent and favour the floatier elements of gothic dress.

In the late 1990s and 2000s, various Wiccan and witch practices became more acceptable in many subcultures, as well as alternative and feminist communities which question patriarchal power structures. Environmental issues, shocks to the system caused by the 2008 financial crisis, wars, Covid and general lack of confidence in government has [all these things] have led many people to look for answers elsewhere, including witchcraft.

Emo: This subset emerged in the 2000s and tended to involve listening to emotional music. The uniform was generally skinny jeans, T-shirts in black, white and red – often striped and featuring bones or broken hearts – bracelets and sweatbands, Converse-style shoes or skater trainers, piercings and, most importantly, the tell-tale fringe swept across the forehead. In the 1990s and early 2000s, baggy jeans and cords had been the trouser of choice for various alternative cultures, but by the end of the decade, tight trousers were favoured by emos.

The 2010s and 2020s saw even more subsets emerge, spurred on by social media networks, where people could delve deep in niches. Goth looks of this era include the closely linked **nu goth** and **pastel goth**. Whilst still using black clothes as a base, they tend to dye their hair a range of colours and wear a variety of casual clothes combined with looks from other subcultures and even mainstream fashion, such as leggings or large sunglasses. Much attention is

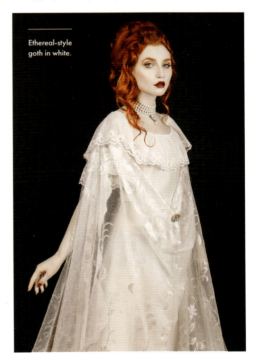

Ethereal-style goth in white.

paid to immaculate hair, make-up and nails – all in gothic shades. The look also borrows heavily from Japanese fashion without going full gothic Lolita. Motifs such as skulls and crosses in bold, graphic designs tend to be favoured.

Gothic grunge has seen a rebirth, teaming gothic looks with the revival of the 1990s grunge fashions, including baggy ripped jeans and plaid shirts.

Dark academia is a social-media–focused subculture involving the enjoyment of classical poetry and gothic architecture. The dress code is a romanticised version of academic dress, with oversized jackets, roll-neck jumpers, baggy cords and waistcoats – but not necessarily in black.

Gothic accessories come in a range of styles, often reflecting a particular subset, and can include Victorian-style reticules, parasols, fans, backpacks adorned with badges and patches showing bands or in shapes such aswings and skulls, chains, spikes and heavy silver jewellery. Crystal balls, Ouija boards, candles, bones, feathers, shells and other items linked to magic spells can also be used as accessories.

Pastel goth girl.

Many goths are just simply goths, rather than belonging to any particular subset. Their wardrobes tend to include long black skirts and trousers, black blouses, sometimes stripy or fishnet tights and long black coats in leather or velvet. Many goths fuse a variety of these styles, or even change styles depending on their mood or social situation.

CONCLUSION

The theme of black runs through gothic fashion. Although now popular in mainstream fashion, it was still being used as a sign of rebellion until the mid- to late twentieth century. It still carries those connotations, as well as being an anti-fashion symbol conveying classic, chic simplicity.

Fighting for one's individuality and right to stand out has become more prominent in the twentieth and twenty-first centuries than ever before. People can now discover like-minded communities and share tastes in music, fashion and leisure, especially on the internet. They can not only move between goth subsets but also even between different subcultures, with society now allowing more time to indulge interests and self-expression.

Goth culture offers escapism and tends to attract kids who do not fit in with the mainstream, sporty culture at their schools. It also provides a safe space for those with an interest in gender experimentation, as goth boys can go for fem-presenting, cross-dressing and androgynous looks, sometimes wearing nail varnish and make-up. Many goths begin life in suburbia before gravitating to bigger cities such as New York or London, where dress codes are not just more relaxed, but quirky fashion sense is actively celebrated.

On the whole, despite often being misunderstood (for example, seen as scary or looked down on for being too soppy), the goth has survived longer than many subcultures. Maybe this is because goth (a bit like punk) is more a state of mind or a way of being than just being about fashion and music.

There have always been People with gothic tastes and demeanour have always sought each other out through a shared interest in fashion, literature or art. While even in subcultures, certain fashions go in and out of style, such as baggy or tight jeans, the goth look has a timeless quality.

For thousands of years, people have been drawn to the past, as well as to the macabre or dark side of folklore; some fear it while others revel in it. It seems unlikely this interest will go away anytime soon.

Selected Bibliography

------◆◆◆------

GOTHIC CULTURE

Baddeley, Gavin, 2010, *Goth: Vamps and Dandies*, London Plexus.

Baddeley, Gavin, 2002, *Goth Chic*, London, Plexus.

Brill, Dunja, 2008, *Goth Culture: Gender, Sexuality and Style*, Oxford, Berg.

Greenwood, Susan, 2011, *The Illustrated History of Magic & Witchcraft*, London, Lorenz.

Hughes, W., Smith, A., eds. (2012) *The Victorian Gothic: An Edinburgh Companion*, (E-book) Edinburgh, Edinburgh University Press, UAL.

Kilpatrick, Nancy, 2004, *The Goth Bible*, New York, St Martin's Press.

Scharf, Natasha, 2011, *Worldwide Gothic: A Chronicle of a Tribe*, published by Independent Music Press of I.M.P. Publishing.

Scharf, Natasha, 2014, *The Art of Gothic*, London, Omnibus Press.

Spooner, C., 2004, *Fashioning Gothic Bodies*, Manchester, Manchester University Press.

Spooner, Catherine, 2006, *Contemporary Gothic*, London, Reaktion Books.

Spooner, Catherine, 2017, *Post-Millennial Gothic: Comedy, Romance and the Rise of Happy Gothic*, London, Bloomsbury.

Taylor, Leila, 2019, *Darkly*, New York, Random House.

Voltaire, 2004, *What is Goth?*, Newbury Port, Weiser Publishing.

Von Teese, Dita, 2006, *Burlesque and The Art of The Teese / Fetish and the Art of The Teese*, New York, Regan Books.

FASHION AND HISTORY

Andrews, Michael, 1991, *The Birth of Europe*, London, BBC Books.

Ashelford, Jane, 1996, *The Art of Dress*, London, National Trust Enterprises Ltd.

Blanks, Tim, 2017, *The World of Anna Sui*, New York, Abrams.

Austen, J., LeFaye, D., Ed., 1995, *Jane Austen's Letters*, 3rd edition, Oxford, Oxford University Press.

https://www.janeausten.co.uk

Cunnington, P., Lucas, C., 1972, *Costume for Births, Marriages & Deaths*, London, A & C Black Ltd.

Cunnington, C.W., Cunnington, P., 1973, *Handbook of English Costume in the 19th Century*, 4th Edition, London, Faber and Faber Ltd.

Cunnington, C.W., Cunnington, P., 1951, *The History of Underclothes*, Mansfield, A.D., Mansfield, V., Reprinted 1981, London, Faber and Faber Ltd.

Downing, S. J. P., (2015) *Fashion in The Time of Jane Austen*, 7th ed. London, Shire Publications.

Evans, G., 2011, *Fashion in Focus 1600–2009: Treasures from the Olive Matthews Collection*, Surrey, Butler, Tanner and Dennis Ltd.

Fraser, F., 1987, *The English Gentlewoman*, London, Barrie and Jenkins.

Fukai, A., Suoh T.,Iwagami, M., Koga R., and Nii R., eds. (2002) *The Collection of the Kyoto Costume Institute Fashion A History from the 18th to the 20th Century*, Milan, Taschen.

Gordon, C., 2016, *Romantic Outlaws: The Extraordinary Lives of Mary Wollstonecraft and Mary Shelley*, Croydon, Windmill Books.

Hamilton Hill, Margaret, Bucknell, Peter A, 1989, *The Evolution of Fashion*, London, B T Batsford Ltd.

Johnson, B., Rothstein, N., ed., 1987, *Barbara Johnson's Album of Fashions and Fabrics*, London, Thames and Hudson.

Johnston, L. P., 2005, *Nineteenth-Century Fashion in Detail*, 2nd Edition, London, V and A Publishing.

Kim, A., Mida, I., 2015, *The Dress Detective*, London, Bloomsbury.

Pool, D., 1994, *What Jane Austen Ate and Charles Dickens Knew*, New York, Touchstone.

Racinet, A., 1888, *The Costume History*, Reprinted 2015, Cologne, Taschen.

Smith, D., 2007, *An Illustrated Encyclopaedia of Uniforms of The Napoleonic Wars*, London, Lorenz Books.

Steele, V., 2007, *The Corset: A Cultural History*, 5th Edition, London, Yale University Press.

Stonell Walker, Kirsty, 2018, *Pre-Raphaelite Girl Gang*, London, Unicorn Publishing.

Taylor, L., 1983, *Mourning Dress: A Costume and Social History*, Herts., George Allen & Unwin (Publishers) Ltd.

Vallance, Aymer, 1989, *The Life and Work of William Morris*, London, Studio Editions.

Vickery, A., 1998, *The Gentleman's Daughter: Women's Lives in Georgian England*, London, Yale University Press.

Walker, R.A., 1948, *The Best of Beardsley*, London, Spring Books.

Waugh, N., 1973, *The Cut of Women's Clothes*, London, Faber and Faber Ltd.

Wilcox, Claire, 2012, *Vivienne Westwood*, London, V and A Publications.

Wise, S., 2005, *The Italian Boy*, London, Pimlico, Random House.

Zacek-Bassett, L., (2016) *Gothic to Goth: Romantic Era Fashion and Its Legacy*, Hartford, Wadsworth Atheneum Museum of Art / University Press of New England.

TV

Make Up: A Glamorous History, BBC, 4th May 2021, 3 Episodes.

PODCASTS

Moon Beaming with Sarah Faith Gottesdiener.

Not Just the Tudors with Suzanna Lipscomb.

The Witch Wave with Pam Grossman.

Betwixt The Sheets with Kate Lister.

MUSEUMS

Bath Fashion Museum, Assembly Rooms, Bennett Street, Bath BA1 2QH.

Blaise Castle House Museum, Henbury Road, Bristol BS10 7QS.

The Blandford Fashion Museum, Lime Tree House, 11 The Plocks, Blandford Forum, DT11 7AA.

The Bowes Museum, Newgate, Barnard Castle DL12 8NP.

Brighton Museum and Art Gallery, 12A Pavilion Parade, Brighton BN1 1EE.

Chertsey Museum, The Cedars, 33 Windsor Street, Chertsey KT16 8AT.

The Fan Museum, 12 Crooms Hill, London SE10 8ER.

The Fashion and Textile Museum, 83 Bermondsey Street, London SE1 3XF.

Keats House, 10 Keats Grove, London NW3 2RR.

Gallery of Costume at Platt Hall, Platt Lane, Manchester M14 6LA.

Strawberry Hill House, 268, Waldegrave Road, Twickenham TW1 4ST.

Royal Pavilion, 4/5 Pavilion Buildings, Brighton BN1 1EE, Visited: 05/07/2017.

The V&A Museum, Cromwell Rd, Knightsbridge, London SW7 2RL.

Whitby Abbey, Abbey Lane, Whitby YO22 4JT.

Worthing Museum and Art Gallery, Chapel Road BN11 1HP.

CEMETERIES

Arnos Vale Cemetery, Bristol.

Brompton Cemetery, London.

Highgate Cemetery, London.

St Pancras Old Churchyard, London.

St Pancras and Islington, London.

St Peter's Churchyard, Bournemouth.

Acknowledgements

To my husband Mark for his support and unwavering belief in this book. To Mum, Dad, Michael, Charlotte, Noah, Danielle, Tom, Ana, Leo for your excitement and belief in this book. To the various and extended O'Donoghues, Godmans, Keagans, Sinclairs and Averys. To Michelle and Sue for our holiday in Whitby. To Silvana for your amazing sewing and firsthand Gothic Fairy Penguin experiences. For all my friends who have partaken in gothy, witchy, vintagey, burlesque delights with me over the years, especially Annabelle, Di, Steph, Selina, Llewella, Lucy, Abbi and Claire. For Sharona for being an amazing proofreader and cheerleader. For the Paper Dolls writing group, especially Jo and Wenna. For the Next Chapter Writing Group, Lesley, Louise and Cler. For my colleagues at Islington Education Library Service. For the staff and tutors at London College of Fashion, as well as curators, costume keepers and museum staff who made the archival research possible. Thank you to Ian, Lucy, Laurence, Katie and everyone else at Unicorn Press (and their freelancers) for working on this project. Apologies if I have missed anyone – thank you to everyone who has helped!

Alamy/Abaca Press: 10 (right); Entertainment Pictures: 124 (left); Ovidiu Hrubaru: 160; ImageBROKER: 8–9; Warpedgalerie: 10 (left); Art Institute of Chicago: 70; BBC Films: 84; British Library: 44, 97; British Museum: 55 (left); Brooklyn Museum: 50 (left); Detroit Institute of Arts: 45; Flickr/Tony Hisgett: 43; Gary Platt: 146; Martin Soulstealer: 146, 147, 150, 151, 153, 165, 167, 169, 170; Getty Images/Fin Costello/Redferns: 138, 139; Gerard Julien: 159; Victor Virgile: 161; iStock/iiievgeniy: 34, 171; Metropolitan Museum of Art: 23 (left), 27, 37, 52, 55 (right), 56, 61, 64, 65, 66, 77, 80, 85, 86, 91 (left), 91 (right), 94 (left), 94 (right), 98, 99, 102 (left), 102 (top), 103 (top left), 103 (top right), 105, 107; Musea Brugge/Groeningemuseum/Art in Flanders: 51 (right); National Gallery of Art, Washington: 33; Nationalmuseum/Erik Cornelius: 75; Rijksmuseum: 22 (top), 22 (bottom), 50 (right), 51 (left), 59, 87, 89, 90, 95, 102–3, 104; Shutterstock/Donna Beeler: 72; FlexDreams: 130; Ironika: 21, 40, 73, 116; Jetrel: 7, 172; Evgeniya Litovchenko: 13, 30, 141; Merydolla: 24–5; Samuel Ponce: 168; Lev Radin: 159; Andrea Raffin: 152; Rangizzz: 2–3; Smiltena: 31; Serghei Starus: 164; Keith Tarrier: 137; Kiselev Andrey Valerevich: 35, 39, 71, 81, 149; Veryulissa: 113; Colin Ward: 15; Zolotarevs: 134–5; Shutterstock Editorial/Ian Dickson: 143; Bukajlo Frederic/Sipa: 158; Dianne Tanner: 11; Victoria & Albert Museum: 32, 49, 60, 69; Walters Art Museum: 19; Yale University Library: 100 (left).

Cover photo: iStock/Kharchenko_irina7

Index

Page numbers in *italics* refer to photographs and artwork.